South Mountain Magic

Tales of Old Maryland

Madeleine Vinton Dahlgren

2002

ISBN 1-59021-003-4

Manufactured in the United States of America.
Cover and interior design by Bill Patton.

 **Lethe**
P R E S S

102 Heritage Avenue, Maple Shade, NJ 08052
lethepress@aol.com / www.lethepress.com

Publishers note:

Madeleine (Sarah) Vinton Dahlgren (1825-1898) was certainly one of the more noted, yet sadly forgotten, women of her time. Born to the influential family of an Ohio congressman, she always remained situated amongst high society.

Widowed at a young age with two small children, she married John Dahlgren, a widower himself with children. Dahlgren was a decorated naval officer and inventor of the artillery used by the U.S.S. Monitor and other ships of that era.

Madeleine served as hostess for the noted Literary Club of Washington, D.C. Journalism and writing were her passions. In her lifetime, she published articles for local papers on her opposing views on suffragism and local issues, and wrote several books, including *Memoirs of Admiral Dahlgren* (1882), a successful book on etiquette, *Etiquette of Social Life in Washington* (1873), a collection of fantastical stories published after her death, *The Woodley Lane Ghost and Other Stories* (1899), and *South Mountain Magic* (1882).

The story behind this book begins in 1876, when, widowed yet again, Madeleine purchased the old South Mountain Inn in Maryland and transformed it into a private summer residence. She fell in love with South Mountain House, writing an essay entitled "Medieavalism in Maryland," which described the estate near the Civil War battleground as a contemporary medieval castle. There, she lived and entertained for over twenty years. A devout Catholic, she had a small chapel built on the grounds.

During her time spent at the estate, Madeleine became fascinated with the legends and superstitions of the locals, many of which were of Germanic descent. Her religious faith adapted to these odd traditions and bits of folklore, encompassing them rather than excluding, as proof of the existence of a Creator and Divine Will. Indeed, there are many passages of the book that are poetic in stating Madeleine's belief. Yet, she does take a certain delight in recounting some of the more sinister stories.

As for South Mountain House, it still stands. The building had once been an inn and returned to its role as a tavern in the 20th century. Today it is one of the finer dining establishments in the state of Maryland. As for the legends that haunt the mountain, this book is their only surviving testament.

PREFACE.

When, some years ago, we became the owner of South Mountain House and some two hundred acres of land surrounding it on the mountain summit, we retained the well-known name of the old hostelry, but converted it into a private residence.

We were led to make the purchase originally, because we were captivated by the beauty of the splendid views in every direction, as well as those to be seen from the historic house itself. The fact that the battle of South Mountain made the ground classic, added greatly, in our appreciation, to the interest of the natural features of the charming landscape. But it was only after a summer residence of several years on South Mountain, that we became aware of the very peculiar and weird character of the beautiful place.

South Mountain House stands at present like an old-manor seat surrounded by tenantry, being the only place of any size on the mountain. It is the radius around which, within a mile, are to be found a circle of cabins occupied by an honest, laborious, but very poor people. These mountaineers are principally of German descent.

Growing out of a familiar acquaintance with their habits of thought and action, the writer gradually learned their superstitions and heard the various narratives to be found in this book. She now presents these extraordinary stories as they were told her, and recounts the practices she believes to be in vogue. The reader will find that they present, if not an instructive, at least a curious collection.

M. V. D.

CONTENTS

Chapter I

THOUGHTS ON THE OCCULT

PRELIMINARY to treating the reader with such a salmagundi of superstitions as South Mountain presents, we beg to make a few serious reflections, which may perchance lead the mind to receive, with at least a certain measure of gravity, the strange collection we have gathered.

Every one, no matter how prejudiced or realistic, must admit that the occult has in all ages attracted the attention of investigating minds, so that it cannot be considered as any evidence of weak judgment, or want of logical perception, to admit surprising facts, the causes of which cannot be perceived. Rather, indeed, is it the exception when we can clearly trace cause and effect in the arcana of Nature.

And why should it be otherwise, placed as we are in a world which is merely an initial step to another state of existence? As an outgrowth of speculations on the mysterious, we have what might be called a school of occult philosophers. Agrippa has several books devoted to such speculations. Fludd has nine volumes of the Cabala under Hebrew characters.

The fidelity with which the Jews have held to their belief in this Cabala is not excelled by their faith in revelation. Indeed, there is nothing improbable in the supposition that the Book of Nature may at one time have been fully opened to Adam when he was created master of all, and held familiar converse with the Creator.

Afterwards, when the supereminent intelligence of this first perfect man became obscured by sin, revelation was still permitted to make known what was needed for spiritual guidance; but man was left to toil and labor for the lost knowledge of Nature's laws.

To continue to explore and unfold these immutable laws must ever form the grand triumph of human intelligence in this life. The universe, being an act of the Divine Will, must possess not only exoteric or known virtues, but likewise esoteric or concealed properties.

In a certain sense, the human, the superhuman, the preternatural, and the supernatural are alike laws of the universe; so that what we call miraculous, is simply the development of a higher law of the Divine Being. The narrow objection of the incredulous, that God would not subvert. His own laws in order to work miracles, has no force whatever in a rational point of view, because these very surprising effects are, after all, as fully a part of the whole plan, as the less complex facts which fall more readily within the scope of the common observation. The average mind only seizes the ordinary course of things, and there limits itself to the smallest possible compass of present material wants. Yet, even athwart the contracted confines of these sense-bound prisoners, flickers a vague instinct of the undefined and the mysterious, like some faint ray from the inner light of consciousness, which may be dimmed, but can never be totally extinguished, by a sensuous life. To search for, to seize, and to hold the almost intangible links connecting the physical and the spiritual universe, should assuredly form one of our most ardent aspirations! Nor can the grave claim a triumph over that soul which has in life thus cast aside the fetters of the senses. We all know that Nature herself is a book, in whose pages we are to seek for knowledge. There we find the most brilliant products embedded in darkness and mystery. We behold in the historic procession innumerable philosophers and sages, ever seeking for that cabalistic lore, which may overstep the boundary line between the known and the unknown, the seen and the unseen.

Mankind has, indeed, continually rebelled against that Divine fiat, imposed after the fall of man, by which Death's portals alone lift the veil that shrouds the future. Yet, in the search for more light, we may well investigate to what extent we may overcome by intelligence the imperfection of our present condition? How far may our spiritual state conquer the present subjugation to matter? Have we reached the ultimate point in this direction, or are we only standing on the threshold? Assuming that God created man perfect, as would be most compatible, inasmuch as he was formed in His own image; but that he was afterwards allowed to lose his birthright through the exercise of His Godlike faculty of free will, we may well ask, How far is it possible to regain these lost perceptions? Or, indeed, are these perceptions lost, or merely darkened?

The annals of the Catholic faith are filled with accredited instances of souls whose heavenly aspirations and pure lives have enabled them to triumph over natural conditions, until the sublimated spirit is lifted into other scenes, where ecstasies, visions, and mystic revelations open the Heavens to view. If the superior consciousness, the soul, can thus anticipate its future here below, why may not the lower perceptive powers also seize some flashes of light, sent forth from that Divine emanation which permeates creation? For do not the enkindling gifts of the artist, the musician, the poet, represent the Divine element, and communicate to the common apprehension their Promethean fire? What are called *presentiments*, for instance, steal upon us as the echo of footfalls on the limit line, and even *coincidences* serve to point the way to some adjustments which we cannot grasp as palpable fact. How often do we not behold a seemingly relentless destiny drive its helpless victim into a mäelstrom of perdition, which the fixed star of faith above him, or even the mariner's compass of experience, might have averted? The mariner's needle shows us matter pervaded by magnetic influence, and should teach us by way of similitude, that our bodies, which enshrine the Divine principle, must be in the highest degree subject to the most occult laws that govern nature. To trace the exact agreements between magnetism and electricity, between so-called *magic* and a clearer knowledge of things at present unseen, may still become the exalted prerogative of science in the future.

The dull loadstone, that sparkles underneath the blow of steel, hides attractive and directive forces which impel human activity to its utmost. Yet, while this attractive power was known to the ancients, the directive property seems not to have been discovered, or at all events utilized, earlier than the thirteenth century. Since then, this magnetic polarity has given an immense impulsion to the nations of the earth. Tracing still a parallel between the dispositions of mankind and the laws of nature, we find that the soft magnet acquires and loses the magnetic principle with equal facility; while steel, which does not readily receive such influence, being once impressed, retains the magnetic force with tenacity. The mute stone would seem thus to mirror the known laws of human character. The same adaptations may be found in the constitution of the human body, which either confers the magnetic power or receives it; and this power, too, as in the magnet of metal, we observe can be produced or destroyed again. We find these qualities apparently in close sympathy with electricity. But, after all, we have as yet no satisfactory theory concerning the causes of magnetic attraction or repulsion.

Could these causes be clearly investigated, might we not hope in a measure to find therein contained the connecting links between the material and the immaterial? While we are constantly increasing our knowledge as to the *manner* of action, yet we are still ignorant of causes. Are these causes unworthy the most serious contemplation of the scientist? In nature we perceive analogies between magnetism and electricity, — the magnetic influence being internal, the electric on the surface. And so do we find the imagination acting like the electric spark on the human soul, evidently enhancing, if not assisting, to produce certain magnetic conditions. This influence is so perceptible that the question has arisen as to how far the imagination may of itself control the nervous and muscular parts of the body. As applied to our present subject, we may well ask if presentiments are simply the effect of the imagination, or if they may find a recognized place in the science of the future.

The connecting links between the real and the unreal can neither be fully traced or defined. They may be said to be represented by symbolism, and the presence of the symbolic exists throughout the universe.

We are told by the scientist that symbolism gives expression to the facts of science; the mathematician makes his abstractions manifest through it; the poet uses the typical as a ladder to reach ethereal heights; the artist wields forms and colors to grasp an ideal; the musician evokes harmonies that echo heavenly refrains; the theologian reads dogmas through faith in things unseen; and the saints rise into seraphic ardors, finding all of Nature but a symbolism of God.

Strangely enough, it is in symbols that man not only finds expression for his ultimate and best conceptions, but he also makes known by symbols his first and rudest wants.

The typical is thus the alpha and the omega of the language of Nature.

We behold the dusky savage holding his belief in the spirit-land awkwardly as a rusty key tarnished through want of use; but with it he stands in the outer darkness, groping ever near those shining gates of knowledge, from whence, perchance, glimmer some faint rays of light. Thus he makes his first essay, until Revelation makes known to him that his vague longings are the realities of a better world.

In symbols the most lofty imagination views the divine plan. In them we accept "the evidence of things not seen."

It is difficult to suppose any state of existence in

which symbolism shall cease to be the reflected glory of the Primal Source. The higher and purer the aspirations of the soul, the more sublime are the visions that lead to a still higher thought. Nor can symbolism find a limit; for, as we have shown, it reaches to the immortal, and the immortal is the eternal.

But as every use has its abuse, so out of these mysteries ignorance wrests its superstitions which the learned may sneer at, but cannot explain.

Chapter II

SOUTH MOUNTAIN HOUSE TRADITIONS

SOUTH MOUNTAIN has become historic on account of the very important battle fought for the command of its passes on September 24th, 1862. The various historians of the Civil War have fully described this struggle, which in history bears the name of "The Battle of South Mountain." The combat was particularly fierce on the heights near and in the vicinity of South Mountain House. General Reno was killed in an open field not a mile distant, and during the entire day the fight was unremitting. Towards sunset the victory rested with the Union troops, and General Lee withdrew his forces during the night. The bloody contest carried on amid these steep and rugged hillsides has invested with a romantic interest, which increases with the lapse of time, the entire pass and the crowning crests overlooking it.

South Mountain is one of the ranges of the Blue Ridge chain that extends from Virginia and continues into Pennsylvania and its numerous lovely shapes and outlines are bathed in the same delicious and peculiar *blue* atmosphere.

Although these heights of which I write scarcely gain two thousand feet of altitude, and are not of Alpine or of Altaic grandeur, and the sparkling variety that water gives to the landscape is wanting, yet the encompassing width of view that the summit glories in is, indeed, most beautiful to behold.

The summer heat on this fair platform of Nature's

framing is tempered by the constant breezes that pass
through the funnel-shaped gorge into which you enter as
you descend the mountain from the east, and which
finally opens out on to a wide and fertile expanse of
valley. It is difficult to realize that these beautiful farm
lands of Washington County, now so smiling and fruitful,
were once ruthlessly ravaged by contending armies. But
even the Antietam has long since given its placid waters
to the arts of peace.

On the mountain top, the constant movement of the
air produces a rarefaction so remarkable that the most
ardent rays of the summer solstice lose their most
oppressive power.

On the other side, the approach from Frederick,
through the famous Middletown valley, across the
beautiful Catoctin hills, up to the glorious historic pass
upon whose summit South Mountain House keeps
faithful watch and ward, is exquisite. The old national
road of wide and now historic fame, and once of great
importance, winds around the base of the mountain,
and cuts its white thread of line by gradual course up
the forest-crowned ascent. Here, from acclivity to plateau,
the trend of the mountain wave is of exceeding grace,
and of mysterious horseshoe form. At last we reach the
few acres of table-land where, on the narrow ridge of top,
stands our loved summer home, "South Mountain
House."

For half a century the old stone tavern has enclosed
within its firm-built edifice many associations that may
well serve to fill the future page of fiction.

Although it has been remodeled and enlarged, yet
the repairs needed to make it a private residence and
comfortable for a summer-home have been so reverently
made, that the antiquated appearance of the place has
rather been enhanced by the deference given to the spirit
of its surroundings.

Here gather around one in the gloaming, evoked from
the record written on these walls, the grandiose forms of
Jackson and Clay who loved to come to this wayside inn,

or in the light foot-fall of the Ellsler fleeing before the gory shapes of wounded men brought hurriedly in amid the fierce heats of battle, while these again flit faintly past, and one hears the hobnail clamp of the sturdy farmer blustering in from the fierce winter cold for a warm drink; or slow and fagged, the wearied step of the belated traveller, seeking a night's shelter from the howling storm. And according to the traditions, when the furious blasts shriek and the gibbous moon grows pale, spectred shapes meet for battle array and moan their requiems, or shrouded ghosts of many shapes troop vaporous to the very door-way.

Of the traditions of the old house we shall now speak.

Once in the early days, when South Mountain was an almost unbroken wilderness, and the rude road scarcely pointed the way through the trackless forest, a company of soldiers arrived at the old hostelry, sadly in need of supper and a night's rest. They were men as hardy as the mountaineer: true "*regulars*," and being marched into the Seminole war. The arms were stacked in the bar-room, where noisy revel already preceded the supper, and most of the soldiers were there in blatant talk with Mine Host.

One man, however, sat motionless near the huge kitchen hearth-stone, the cheery flame of the hickory sapling leaped up the big-throated chimney, where the coffee-pot boiled over the rousing fire, and savory slices of bacon simmered, giving their appetizing flavor to the newly-laid eggs frying in the pan. The famous "Maryland biscuits" were baking in crisp and fleecy rolls, while chickens were broiling over the red-hot coals.

Brisk and busy were the swift fingers of the tavern-keeper's daughter Saidee, and bright were her flashing black eyes, contrasting with the glowing cheeks, as she got ready this toothsome meal.

Still and intent on every movement, the soldier gazed.

He was a handsome fellow, of compact, well-built frame; Saxon light hair and blue eyes, and he came from the lake-girdled forests of Michigan. Hardship and he were boon companions, and, up to this time, little reckoned this "Soldier Boy" as to what might betide.

But his hour had come, and an arrow more piercing, more fatal, than any Seminole sped from his noisome swamps, had transfixed him to the heart. *He was in love!* Oh, gruesome fate, to have met this "bonnie lassie" only to know the pain of parting for the early morning's hateful tramp!

Inadvertently he groans aloud when Saidee, who had, despite her earnest work, felt the magnetic power of the earnest blue eye so intently fixed upon her, suddenly turned and said: "And what's the matter, man? I rather reckon you be tired, right smart." "Saidee," said the soldier in a low, sad voice, "I wish I'd got to *die* for you!" A high-backed wooden settle had its place in the chimney-corner, and on this Saidee instantly dumped down, with such an utter look of sheer surprise, mixed with a sort of angry disdain, as she tossed her head: "*Die* for me, Mister! Well, ain't I worth *living* for?" "Living for!" exclaimed the soldier, grasping her unreluctant hand, "A thousand lives, if I had them; but I can only give you one." The old adage says, "Truth is strange, stranger than fiction," and the truth of this story is, that in the watches of that night, when "love at first sight" had told "the old, old story," it was planned between this love-lorn pair, that the soldier should *desert*. He would secrete himself in the pathless forest of the gorge, where, watching from overhanging cliffs, he could keep clear of his pursuers; and that Saidee would, hovering not far off, if need be imitate the cry of the wildcat and let him know when danger was near; that when she brought him food, she would place it on a certain rock, hidden by overhanging trees, and where any slight noise would be lost in the confusing sound of a not distant waterfall; that thus they would bide the time until pursuit had ended, when he would come out of hiding-place, build him a cabin on the mountain, and take Saidee for his bride. Thus the early morning finds this victim of the "insatiate archer," *a deserter*! The company of soldiers soon discover their loss, but their captain is loathe to believe that William could desert. Saidee suggests that he has lost his way in the forest on the cliffs back of the house. All day is lost looking for him. Another and another day, ever misled, ever searching in vain.

At last, after spending three or four days, they conclude that he has, poor fellow, come to grief; they can no longer delay, and the onward march is taken.

Meantime, a faint glimmer as of some fire is now and then seen by the mountaineer in some dark depth of the gorge, and strange cries as of some prowling wildcat are heard in remote places. At last it is safe to leave the hiding-place; all is told, laughed over, and forgiven, and the lovers live and die in their mountain hut. But yet to this day, the romance of the wooing has not worn away, and the story is told and retold with renewed zest. Nor does it stop there, for it is thought by some that, oft and again, the wraiths of these two repeat the cunning device. At midnight the soldier's distant fire may be seen lighted, or the stealthy step of the winsome Saidee is heard, who makes known her approach by giving the peculiar cry of the wildcat, in order to frighten away the curious.

This story was told us by a very distinguished man, while our guest at South Mountain House, to whom it was narrated in his boyhood by an old soldier, one of the company who searched for the missing man, and who learned after many years the real truth of the whole matter. "And," added our friend as he sat musing in a reclining chair of the quaint wainscoted library, the diamond-shaped panes of the casement casting checkered lights upon the ash and walnut floor, "how passing strange that in this very room which was the old bar-room of the hostel, I should be here to repeat this story, to which I listened as a far-off tale in my youth!"

South Mountain House lies cradled on a spot of ground so narrow that, to build its length of seventy-five feet, the hill had to be cut into somewhat. This in turn necessitated a walled court-yard of considerable size around the rear entrance, into which you descend by a flight of stone steps.

The crags back of the house are superb, and precipitous, and form a ledge of fine cliffs. Near the summit of this ridge, a small level space of perhaps thirty by fifty feet, marks the spot where the Southerns planted artillery in order to command the pass, previous to the battle. From this "signal station," which is perhaps a hundred feet higher than the house, the slope downward is very graceful.

The hill side is threaded by numerous paths, seats are placed where vistas open, and there is a rustic arbor, deeply shaded by a luxuriant wild grape-vine, and overshadowed by majestic trees.

The sunset view is best enjoyed from a lovely grove, where ledge after ledge of sparkling quartz-rock form natural terraces. Their rugged surfaces gleam in the moonlight and, as seen from the house, assume fantastic shapes, amid the confusing disorder of wind-tossed overhanging boughs of surrounding trees.

The house fronts near the old National Road, and, across this road and divided by an osage orange hedge, is an open ten-acre field of clover — but, oh, how very beautiful it is! — inclining gently downward, amphitheatrical in contour, fringed in by a wealth of wild vines and shrubs, outlined by pine forests of dark and sombre hue, rising then to the height of corresponding cliffs on the other side, which we have described, and giving here, there, everywhere, as an enrapturing outlook, an extent of fifty miles of scene. The eye ranges afar over both valleys that open to view from either side.

And yet, such is the grim mockery of sin's burden on

this fair world, that, during the memorable September 14th, over this beauteous slope the dreadful tide of battle swept the lifelong day. Here then, surging and resurging waves of men held each other in mortal combat, until what was in the morning light a glowing corn-field had become, by "dewy eve," a trodden down and begrimed mass of desolation, incumbered with hundreds of dead.

Nor yet did the carnage stop with this holocaust; for, on the glorious summit beyond the pines and stretching over many a field, the hundreds swelled into thousands. What wonder then, when the pallid moon glints faintly through the stately pines, or the stars keep faithful watch, or the mantling darkness covers the ground like a pall, that awful shapes arise, sentinels hold solemn conclave, and mystic lights are traced. Eastward, the imagination takes a still wider range, for the declivity of the mountain side blends in perplexing irregularity with the distant landscape.

It was Hallowe'en, crisp and clear cold; and towards midnight the moon, that in the early evening had struggled to free herself from obscuring clouds, shone forth unclouded. The household were all abed and asleep, with the exception of two members, who, each in their separate rooms, were reading. One of these rooms opened by a casement window on to a covered veranda, which overlooked the view eastward. At some distance from the house in that direction, and half-hidden by the sloping ground, is a fine stone barn, whose vermilion-red roof, as seen through vistas of trees, gives warmth and contrast of coloring to the landscape. The attention of the occupant of this room was arrested by what seemed to be a strong sulphurous odor. The idea at once occurred that some malicious tramp had set fire to the barn. When, stepping quickly out upon the porch, this apprehension was increased almost to a certainty by observing something like thin wreaths of curling smoke in that direction; while the peculiar odor was still more perceptible in the open air.

Fearing that there might indeed be a stifled fire, and no time to be lost, the alarm was very quietly given to the other person, who was still up. No one else was disturbed, but the two then proceeded to the observatory on the top of the house, from whence the appearance of smoke was directly visible, as well as the sulphurous smell, which was unmistakable.

Now really alarmed, and feeling sure that some nefarious attempt was in progress of execution, a trusted man-servant was aroused, and sent with a loaded revolver to investigate matters.

After some twenty minutes of time, during all of which the same condition of things continued, the man came back grumbling.

He said he had looked everywhere, explored the grounds, gone beyond the barn, which he had examined, proceeded as far as the gardener's house, —and all was still and safe. So off to bed he pattered, muttering something about being "waked up for nothing at all."

Surprised and more puzzled than ever, the two watchers returned to the veranda.

The moon now threw out brilliant streams of light, and every object was diaphanous in her opaline atmosphere. At this precise time, *midnight* held the even balance of the hours, and a never-to-be-forgotten scene developed itself.

The circlets of smoke took on a vaporous glamour, but yet defined as if opaque. Some moments later, numerous *shrouded wraiths* marshalled in mid-air on the brow of the declivity. Presently they ranked in approaching columns, with a swaying movement. A flash of intelligent apprehension seized both lookers-on, for now there was no mistaking the illusion of *phantom hosts* forming for conflict!

As suddenly this opposing embattled phalanx swayed with a forward movement towards the house, both exclaimed, as if inspired by one breath, *"The battle smell!"* Too affrighted to pause another moment, they rushed back into the room, and closed out all vision of what had become too appalling to gaze upon.

This is no fancy sketch, but a description, as exact as words can make it, of what actually transpired, both of the spectators of this wonderful phantasm possessing cultivation above the average measure of intelligent powers of discrimination.

Afterwards, thought and speculation only "made the wonder grow," for these strange facts presented themselves. It was, curiously enough, All Hallowe'en, the very night above all others given over by common superstition to spectral apparitions. Yet this fact had played no part in enkindling the imagination, because it was only remembered in discussing the strange event afterwards. Moreover the wonderful culmination actually did take place *exactly at midnight.*

Then, most astonishing of all, two senses were affected, sight and smell; for added to distinct vision was the pervading odor, that sulphurous battle-smoke that had first perplexed and aroused the attention! And then came the still more curious fact, that the man who went through the grounds on a tour of investigation failed to notice anything at all.

Was it the finer sense, the keener perception, or the more hallucinated imagination of the two, that enabled them to witness a spectacle hidden from a third person of a coarser nature?

We may have a theory, but we refrain from the attempt to do more than to give this narrative as clearly as possible.

A pleasant little circle had passed a cheerful evening in the library of South Mountain House. There were two gentlemen whose conversation was especially instructive.

It was exhilarating to listen to the playful contest of assured and ready scholars, relieved by an inexhaustible fund of anecdote. One of these two men was a venerable age, and, added to the most extensive acquirements, had a profound knowledge of the world. But so winning was his nature that the positions of honor and trust he had so well filled had only served to give him a more expansive feeling of Christian benevolence towards humanity.

His was the noble presence of an old age, where a life of excellence had but served as a preparation for the glowing and abundant harvest that the radiant sunset garnered in.

It was at a late hour that the venerated guest bade good-night to his friends, who at once sought their respective rooms.

One of this social circle occupied the chamber called "the red room," that commanded a magnificent view westward, and also overlooked the clover-field which once had witnessed such dreadful scenes.

But without other thought than a consciousness of fatigue, the lady seated herself beside an open casement. The night was sultry; yet its oppression had not until then been realized, and, with a weariness she could scarcely account for, she leaned forward in the deep recess of the window to catch a fresher and more cooling air. The sky was of that inky blackness that is at times noticed when the greatest summer heat prevails. Suddenly, to her great surprise, she beheld a portion of the house, which on this side projects into a tower, illuminated with a bright light thrown upon it. Is it possible, she thought, that in this climate the Aurora Borealis should assume such exceeding brilliancy? One would rather suppose it to be the reflected light of the constellation called the Southern Cross. Looking upward, there was nought but blinding darkness: not even a star was visible in the blackness of the firmament. Then a glance towards the field at once made manifest the cause of the brightness.

For not over fifty yards distant, standing out in the

National Road, was an apparition, possibly eight feet in height, and of the ordinary breadth of the human frame. It was shrouded, statuesque, immobile, yet not shadowy, but of distinct outline. Emanating from it, and as it were a part of its substance, proceeded a bright white light. This light formed the atmosphere that surrounded it, and, being reflected against the wall of the wing of the house, was first noticed.

No second look was taken, but Heaven's aid invoked and the casement quickly closed.

Observing her watch, the hands indicated the precise moment *of midnight!*

After breakfast the next morning, lounging in the music room, where a glass door of stained and diamond-shaped panes casts a mystic hue, the incident of the previous night was narrated. The recital was gravely listened to and without comment. There was a pause. No one spoke; and the lady could no longer restrain the question: as addressing her wise and aged friend, she bluntly asked, "Do you believe in ghosts?"

"I do," was the solemn answer. But not another word would he utter on this subject.

And as the balmy air was filled with fragrance of the wild-rose, the woodbine, and clematis, it seemed, amid the renewed and mirthful chat and the bright, real life of the morning, as if naught unsubstantial had a place, at least in the sunshine of this beautiful world.

The summer had passed away, and another had succeeded it. The incident we have related had never again been spoken of, when one night the hostess heard a light nervous tap at her door. A little lady, who had been of the household the summer previous, stood before it trembling.

"Pardon," she said, "if I disturb you, madam, I had to come—for—I have seen a ghost!"

"A ghost, my child. Why, what can you mean?

Sit down, just here in this easy-chair. Pray, were you dreaming?"

Well, the story was soon told.

The room occupied by this guest commanded nearly the same view as on that other occasion we have described. As she stood by the open casement, she saw this shrouded figure in the grounds, some thirty yards from the house, and perhaps about the same distance from where it had been noticed a year before. It was evidently a repetition of the same phantom, from the description, although only a momentary look had been given. It was surrounded by the same peculiar white light, that emanated from it in all directions.

As the recital was finished, the old English clock, that stands erect as a sentinel, reaching up to the ashen beams of the dining-room ceiling, with measured strokes told twelve — *midnight.*

It was agreed that no mention should be made to the family of the event of the night.

Some weeks later and the visit of the little lady to this mountain home was about to close, and she was to leave in the very early morning. Although she had bidden adieu to the various members of the family, the hostess was prompted to go to her room at a late hour, to ask if anything additional could be done to make more comfortable the mountain drive to be taken at break of day.

As the two ladies stood at the open casement that looked westward towards the mystic grove, scanning the outer darkness, the recollection of the mysterious apparition that had twice been seen caused one of them suddenly and involuntarily to lean out of the window and exclaim: "*What was it* that appeared? Could it have been *a lost soul*?"

Scarcely were these words uttered, when with the rapidity of the vivid lightning there flashed forth at some yards' distance, suspended in mid-air, *two phosphorescent wings*, which, for an instant only, fluttered wildly open, as if some wounded dove had extended its pierced plumage, and then as instantly closed them rigidly fixed, dissolving back into the deep gloom from whence it came.

"Let us close the shutters and commend ourselves to God," shuddered the ladies, as at the very instant the metallic notes of the encoffined timepiece below struck *midnight!*

A lady much fatigued by travel arrived at South Mountain House. She occupied a room called "the Blue Room," on account of the color that pervades the apartment. Being very tired and sleepy, she retired at an early hour, but the moment her weary head touched the pillow, a door which opened into her room very near the bed, was shaken with some force. After a few minutes of attentive listening, she became aware that the manner in which the door shook indicated an intelligence which directed the movement at regularly recurring intervals. It would shake three distinct times, with just enough of intermission to mark the space of time. Then there would be a considerable pause, when the door would again shake, precisely as before. This was intolerable, and defied sleep. So she examined the door very carefully, even opened it while shaking, and looked into the hall. All was dark and still. But upon closing the door the same phenomenon was repeated. She began to be alarmed, and an undefined dread of being alone seized upon her. So she aroused one of the maids of the house, and asked her if she would stay all night on a couch in the room. The obliging girl came at once, and was soon fast asleep. After a period of intent listening, during which there was no repetition of the sound, the lady fell asleep, nor did she awaken until morning, when she was disturbed by the stir of the woman, who was up and was leaving the room.

The superb locust-trees shading the window to the

east, filled the air with the fragrance of their bloom; and the song of birds amid their branches, as they greeted the newly risen sun, was jubilant. As the roseate light diffused its cheerful influence through the Blue Room, the lady felt quite ashamed that she should have been so nervous the night before, and she begged the maid to make no mention to the family of the circumstance.

The day was spent in the various rural pleasures a country home offers, and walks, drives, rides, and open-air games, all in the exhilarating mountain air brought wholesome bodily fatigue by night. Not-with-standing this weariness, no sooner had her head rested on the pillow than the door began to shake precisely as on the night before. Too nervous to endure this renewed demonstration, the maid was at once sought, and a second time spent the night in the room, and, as on the former occasion, all was quiet after the woman joined her, and again she enjoyed a night of undisturbed repose. The lovely morning anew dispelled the uncomfortable illusions of the night, and the request was repeated to the servant not to mention her timidity.

That day an excursion in an open country wagon was made to a spot called the Black Rock, some miles distant, that commanded a wonderful view. The jolting over rough roads had induced fatigue, while the hilarious excitements of the day had entirely dissipated any dread of the coming night. So, pleasantly disposed for dream-less slumber, for the third time she sought a quiet night in the Blue Room, only for the third time to notice the same disturbance, and for the third time to ask the protection of the maid. The next day she confessed that she was afraid to sleep in the Blue Room at night alone, and asked that a little daughter of her friend might be allowed to share the room with her. This request was granted, and the unusual occurrence ceased.

To our apprehension the most striking fact in this recital is, that whatever the nature of the mysterious appeal thus made, it was evidently intended *for this one lady, and for no other person*, for the presence of a companion in the room was sufficient to secure exemption from annoyance.

Doubtless the spiritist who may read this will claim the incident as one very familiar, and will deem the explanation easy, viz., that this lady was selected, on account of being a good "medium," to communicate some intelligence from the spirit world, and that whenever another person was present, the magnetic rapport needed for the communication was destroyed. But as it is our present purpose rather to tell stories than to explain them, we have no comment to make.

The mother of the family was absent, and the children, feeling lonesome, had taken refuge in the large airy laundry for an hour of the early evening. The various labors of the day being at an end, the domestics had assembled therein, as was their wont, for an hour's chat in the gloaming, and a ripple of talk was going on among the maids. The stolid Dutch farmer sat smoking his pipe, and near him were grouped the children, quiet because weary from the continuous play of a long midsummer's day. The twilight had so gradually deepened into obscurity that no lamps had been lighted.

The room was of large size — some thirty by twenty feet — and had six windows and several doors. The outside door opened out upon the lawn, and within one led into the family dining-room, another into the kitchen, and yet another into a small hall, where a stairway leading to the rooms of the domestics terminated. Since then this large room has been torn down and replaced by another structure. In this commodious old-fashioned hall, which had originally been built for a ballroom, where summer boarders could disport themselves, but which, when the house became a private residence, was used as a sort of servants' hall, — here, in the uncertain crepuscular light, the household were congregated.

Presently, *something* was heard to enter the open door-way, and its gliding progress was *felt* but not *seen*. As it passed onward into the dining-room, a distinct clatter as of hoofs could be heard, which made its way through the kitchen, back again amid the affrighted group of listeners, from whence it could be traced first in the vestibule and then ascending the stairway — step by step — clank, clank, — then dying away in the remote attic.

Recovering from the momentary panic, the lamps were quickly lighted, the maids armed themselves with broomsticks, pokers, shovels, and tongs; the children got whips, an old rusty sabre found on the battle-field, and a boy's knife; while the farmer went for his loaded musket. The three dogs were called in to aid in the search, and an indescribable and exciting investigation commenced of the entire house — from cellar to topmost closet. If an uncertain shadow fell on the floor it got a thwack; if a curtain fluttered in the evening breeze it was beaten; garments hanging in wardrobes were poked into, and even the beds got a swinging rap to test them.

The boys trooped on with an encouraging halloo in front, and the Dutchman brought up the rear with his blunderbuss pointed blank at the party before him. What a disappointment! The dear old house bore the brunt of the storm and came out of the squall like a fine ship, rigged, never for a moment thrown on her beam-ends, and with colors flying. "Dear me," cried Jack, "it's too bad that scaly monster got away!"

"Let us all go to mother's room, anyhow," cried the children in chorus. "Nothing will dare to go THERE. It is the safest place."

So, tumultuously, they all took refuge in the mother's room, nor did any one venture to separate from the other. There, ensconced, were children, servants, and dogs, only the Dutchman kept guard at the door of the room, with his lighted pipe and his rusty musket.

And as the night wore on, no one stirred, no, not even a mouse!

And the mother — she had gone to Frederick to
attend to some business, taking the cars thither, and
expecting to return in the stage that would pass the
house at four in the afternoon on the next day. She was
accompanied by a guest, a young lady who was making
a visit at the mountain home.

All business having been attended to, the ladies went
to the City-Hotel, intending to remain there until the
departure of the stage the next day. They had taken tea,
and already the night had set in rather dark. Suddenly,
the matron spoke to her young friend:

"I cannot explain why, Alice. I know it is foolish, but
I feel uneasy about my children, who are left alone with
the servants; and I think I will hire a close carriage and
go home to-night. Are you afraid, my dear, to take this
mountain drive of fourteen miles alone with me in a
strange conveyance, and guided by a driver of whom we
know nothing. I think we can reach South Mountain
House by midnight."

After a little pause Alice answered, "I can scarcely say
that I am afraid, and yet, if you will allow me to speak
plainly, madam, I am surprised that you should change
your plans, without apparent reason, and risk so venture-
some a drive by night, to say nothing of what seems to
me incurring a considerable and needless expense."

"All that you say, Alice, is perfectly true, but if you are
not afraid, we will go."

So the hack was hired, and the driver was recommended as safe and responsible. By eight o'clock the
historic bridge of Frederick-Town, close by Barbara
Frietchie's house, had been passed, and the ladies were
soon in the open country. Presently the faint traces of
light faded into utter darkness. At times the horses would
pause, as if unable to feel the way. But they kept a steady
pace, and now and then the glimmer of some lamp
marked a not distant house. Then again the barking of

dogs greeted them, as they drove past still other farms. But by the time the long, slanting range of the Catoctin was ascended and descended, they plunged forward in sheer darkness.

Middletown gave no sign of life as they passed through it, but it was pleasant to know that only five more miles had to be made.

The tedious ascent of South Mountain seemed interminable. But by midnight the summit had been gained, and as the moon began to give some glinting rays, the dim outline of the old gray stone house could just be discerned.

"Here at last, thank Heaven!" sighed the lady, who, in the weariness of the long, dismal drive, had reproached herself mentally again and again, to have exposed her companion as well as to have herself incurred such needless risks, led by a mere impulse, — an impulse, too, she could neither explain nor account for.

At the last moment it flashed upon her mind that they would have to risk the first onset of the dogs, before they could sufficiently arouse the sleeping household to gain a shelter. But it was too late to hesitate, for at this moment they stopped at the main entrance of the house. Almost in a twinkling, and before they had fairly gotten out of the carriage, to their utter amazement, the entire household — children and servants — rushed out pell-mell to welcome their return, except indeed the Dutchman, who was too phlegmatic to run.

"Why, my children! Well Mary, Ellen, Jane and Betsy, what does it all mean? And you too, Hans? Mercy on us! Don't point that musket this way! And Spot, Jack, and Prince in the house, too! Most astonishing!"

When the explanation of the wonderful hubbub was given, the mother laughed so long that the rolling tears had to be wiped from her cheeks, and the boys reddened and began to feel hurt. "Why, boys, fie! I never said it was an old rat, for that would have gone bang — flop — flippety-flop!" and again she laughed. "Of course it was not a rat, boys, because this 'thing' went 'clank-clank, hoof-hoof!'"

"But, mother, pray tell us," asked Bernard, in his grave, thoughtful way," what was it brought *you* home in this queer manner, at midnight?"

"Well, children, you cannot understand it, but it was really a *presentiment* I had that all was not right at home, that brought me here."

"Oh! It is just splendid!" fairly shouted Jack, the blue-eyed boy, who thirsted for adventure. "While we were having a glorious old time, why, here's the little mother, fourteen miles away, had a *pre-sen-ti-ment!*"

As he spoke, and as if awakening echo answered the youth from out the weird old dining-room, where the blended colors of the mellow woods, and the ashen beams of the beautiful ceiling over-shadow and the quaint Elizabethan casements and fireplace speak of the past — there, where the grandfather's clock stands bolt upright to its work, ever steadily facing the old cupboard that so proudly holds the great grandmother's crystal and china (with the cracked old plate that came over from England more than a hundred years ago) — there rang forth the clangor of its solemn voice of warning that so oft before had counted, as now once again *midnight*.

CHAPTER III

TRADITIONS OF THE INDIAN

AND now adieu to the fanciful romance that invests South Mountain House with the charm of the unseen. We may almost say a sad farewell to the exaltation of the imagination with which we love to welcome the beautiful nature surrounding us, for our theme must now be of the savage, of spooks, and of sorcery.

If, as we have seen, South Mountain House has its traditions, these are of gentle nature compared with all around it; for South Mountain itself is steeped in an atmosphere of superstition from base to summit. These practices and idle fancies are so manifold, curious, hideous, and absurd, that we are puzzled how to unravel the labyrinthine threads of such a maze.

We find, the more we inquire, however, vestiges of the various superstitions of other countries; although the shape they have taken here seems to be of growth indigenous to the Mountain. It is, indeed, well known to all who have investigated the history of the world's belief in similar subjects, that under innumerous forms of manifestations of the curious and the mysterious have appeared in all countries and been handed down throughout the ages.

The most astounding exhibitions probably occur in the vast and dreamy Orient, where for thousands of years man has theorized unassisted by revelation. There he revels in the wonders of magic.

The West then introduced in the pagan systems of the

Greeks and Romans so many forms of divination,
that these became a religious creed by which to guide
conduct.

After the oracular voices were stilled by the coming of
the Redeemer, faint echoes still lingered among the
nations, and the Scandinavian, the Saxon, the Teuton, the
Gaul handed down the gross admixture to the Northman,
the German, the Scotch, the Irish, and the French.

The infiltration had by some mysterious process
reached the savage world discovered by Columbus, and
traces of this common bond were also found in the
discovered islands of the seas. Now what is it, that sits
thus enthroned over matter back through the mists of
the ages, and which defies the speculations of modern
science? Or whose real meaning was unread by the
sibyls?

It is, assuredly, *the immortal principle in man*, that ever
reverently does homage to the invisible.

Although man, when unassisted by revelation, grovels
in the abject bonds of the senses, yet even in this darkened prison the principle lurks, reflecting that dual life,
if I may so express it, which is ours: that body and soul
inseparably united in this world, but so very soon to be
separated in the next. Here the caged soul is ever
conscious, ever reaching out of the obscurity of the
senses to the ideal, the unseen world it is so soon to
enter. Of course, only the less important faculties are
developed in this world, because in the immortal life
hereafter all that is needed will be made manifest.

Scarcely hidden from view, as one begins to descend
the western slope towards Boonsboro', and at a turn in
the road, is a collection of log cabins marked down in the
war maps as "Zittle's Town."

Here vegetate some scores of souls, nées Zittles,
married to Zittles, related to Zittles, or connected with

Zittles. Amid these humble homes, and in other similar huts further down on the slopes, or in the ravines that intersect them — some of these cabins almost buried in forest depths, as well as others perched on cliffs beyond — ignorance, tainted by belief in magic, has taken the unearthly form of superstition. Nature, among these simple and un-lettered folk, snatches a language out of her own arcana. What has taken place in consequence goes to disprove any theory of evolution, for the reverse law has held. We find that man left uninstructed has not had his mental facilities developed in an increasing ratio by the fact that he is left at liberty to explore and read the page of nature before him, all lovely as it is; but he has rather grown imbruted and yielded to the grossest impressions of the senses.

He has in this way given to the whims of a degraded fancy that credence alone due to religious faith. The astonishing delusions we are about to speak of are by many held as facts, and are held as matters of serious belief. The incidents have been related to us at various times by different people, with every evidence of personal faith.

We make no apology for exposing the credulity we are about to chronicle, and although we may be tempted to speculate in a philosophical sense upon the origin or the causes of this condition of things, yet we refrain.

It is, however, quite certain, that mysterious causes and mysterious effects are accepted, and, it is confidently asserted, produced. Of these causes and their corresponding effects, we shall, so far as we can, pick up the obscure connection; and to chronicle these narratives will form our theme of *"Mountain Magic."*

In the early times, when all the ranges of mountains still remained an untrodden wilderness, and the aborigines roamed undisturbed over their whole extent, there were thrilling adventures, and the recollection of the terrible cruelty of the savage overshadowed the fairest landscapes.

One old woman told us that after her father had

cleared off a little patch of ground and built his log cabin in the woods, one day he hid himself from view on catching a glimpse of a party of Indians coming along in a hurry. Of the number was a squaw, who tottered along under too heavy a burden for the rapid and continuous march, as she bore, strapped upon her back, a stout child of some four or five years of age. She lagged in the rear of the little band.

Suddenly the chief stepped back, and seizing the child rudely snatched him from the poor mother's back, and dashing him to the ground, drove a pointed stake through the body of the writhing innocent, leaving him pinned to the earth, all heedless of the agony of the mother. Then as quickly the ruthless march was resumed, and the heart-broken woman, thus savagely relieved of her precious load, urged rapidly forward.

The appalled backwoodsman did not dare to emerge from his hiding-place until these fiends were out of sight. He then hastened to the hapless victim and found the boy stiff and stark, dead, and firmly transfixed. The ghastly corpse was carefully buried, out of the reach of the vulture, the wild-cat, and the wolf.

A sad story is also told of a pioneer who had ventured into the wilderness with his wife and four fine children, in order to wrest out of the primeval forest a home and support for his family. He had built the needed log cabin, and around it was already cleared a small piece of ground for the corn and potatoes.

It would indeed seem as if, having grappled with the worst, he might begin to hope for a certain degree of comfort.

One day he took his two boys, leaving the two younger children with the mother, and went into the forest at some distance to work.

During his absence, a band of Indians passing by

swooped down upon the peaceful home, tomahawked the two little girls, and carried away the mother as prisoner.

All unaware of the swift desolation that had overtaken his home, presently with cheery whistle, as he half listened to the babbling boys and half expected the eager welcome of wife and babies, he came upon the promiscuous ruin.

The grief that shrivels, blasts, and withers, yet spares life. So, for seven weary, toilsome years the man plodded on. The corn was planted, and his two boys were ever with the desolate father.

During all this length of time, his heart hungered to know the fate of the wife and mother; but never was the gloom that hung over the forest hut lifted for one moment by an inkling of her fate, or the least glimmer of light to relieve the strain of that awful suspense.

It was early November, and the night was chill on the mountain. A light snow had fallen, the first of the season. As the wind drearily moaned, it suited well the brooding pain in the man's heart. He sat beside the huge fire that the boys, now well grown, had just fed with a fresh hickory log.

The man looked careworn and bent with toil. The never-ceasing battle-brunt of heart and body he had so manfully borne all these years, had left him like the gnarled oak the tempest loves to toss and twist if it cannot break. The youths had reached their fifteen and seventeen years. They were ruddy, well grown, and of lithe and sinewy frames; but even upon their young faces sat the shadowy expression of a heavy grief. They knew well the weight on the father's heart, and they exchanged a look of pity, as they observed his fixed and wistful gaze upon the glowing embers.

"Father," said Willie, "I am now seventeen, and yet it seems to me only as yesterday, that awful day when Sally and Jane were killed — and — mother taken from us."

"Poor mother!" echoed James.

As the hard and horny hand of the poor man brushed away the big rolling tears, a still deeper sigh seemed to linger in the gloaming, and the fitful gust to shake the door. They started: it was so near and real.

"The clinks of this cabin are too open, boys, for the winter's wind: to-morrow we must fill them."

"My father, look!" and the boys jumped to their feet as the latch-string was pulled, the door opened, and there stood before them a shadowy form — so wan, so thin, so deadly pale. Held for one instant in awful suspense, the man gazed in speechless terror, for at the next moment, with long and piercing shriek, the wife and mother had fallen in a dead swoon to the floor! And at her side stood a noble dog, still and composed as if he too, understood it all. "Quick, help, boys! Oh, God of mercy, it is — it is — the mother!" and they bring her back to life, — with all the care that devoted love can give.

The revulsion from the ecstasy of joy, the delirium of happiness, was more than her worn and shattered frame could bear. She only rallied to sink again, and during the long winter gradually, but surely, declined.

In the early spring, with tender and reverent hands, they laid her to rest beside her murdered darlings, where loving hearts had years before adorned the spot, and planted the wild-rose.

During the prolonged illness, the whole sad story was told — little by little, as she could endure to speak of it. On that first dread day, she was hurried on with the Indians, They never molested her, did not treat her with cruelty, but always guarded her with strict care as a prisoner. She was never really trusted. If they were on the march, she was hurried on, and wherever they were, she was always fastened by a stout thong at night to a stake well driven in the ground. Although unmolested, yet she was constantly given to understand that any attempt to escape would cost her, her life.

And yet in the bitterness of all these seven years but one hope sustained her, the wish, the thought, the determination to get back to the dear husband and the two boys and the two graves. As the long-deferred hope deepened into despondency, and the benumbing weight pressed upon her, she felt more and more that, whenever the supreme moment of her deliverance from a captivity worse than death was to come, that it must only be her fate to die among her own. And this last desire was granted her, this wish, that grew out of her amazing suffering, which she had learned to look upon as a boon, was hers.

There was a splendid dog, the pride of the chief, and she had, in many quiet, kindly ways, won him as a friend. And there was of the band an old squaw who took heart of compassion on her. And so it was, when the fullness of her probationary time had come, that one day this Indian woman said to her:

"Pale-face, tonight I will free you from your bonds. I will cut your thong, and you may go free. You may take the dog who is your friend, and he will guard you, and you will face the sun and travel for ten days, until the shadow of South Mountain falls over the Potomac. There, where the river cuts the hill in twain, you are near your home. I will mislead our braves, who will seek the dog, and who would kill you, — and you will not let the grass breathe under your feet. Pale-face, go back to your own, for I see that soon the Great Spirit will call you to the cloud-land."

And so it came to pass the weary march ended in safety; but the wife and mother wandered home — to die, — and to this day, when the story is told, it is with sorrowing pathos.

Aunt Patty's stories!

Now, that we would hear all about the red man, who in the olden time roved, "through wood, through waste, o'er hill, o'er dale," we must first listen to the voice of the aged. We will go and see Aunt Patty, and she will tell us all the mystic legends of this far-away past.

Aunt Patty is now eighty-six years of age. Not long since she consented, for a small stipend, to have some of her neighbors take out an insurance upon her life. After this was effected, she became restless among these mercenary friends, and determined to change her home. So, without making known her intention to any one, this octogenarian started off quite alone and on foot. She walked the entire distance of five mountain miles, to the house of her younger sister, who is only eighty-three, with whom she says she means to end her days. The long and toilsome effort somewhat fatigued her, but she was in no wise injured by the exertion. The two sisters are well content to be together.

Doubtless, notwithstanding the great age of this vigorous woman, those speculators who have staked their money on the hazard of her continuous life will yet be kept waiting many a year; for Aunt Patty looks as if she would assuredly count her years to a full century. She is of unusual size, and has a muscular frame, which age has made sinewy. She wears a brown calico dress, with a full, short skirt, and over this an ample and very wide black alpaca apron that reaches nearly to the hem of her gown. A plain white cotton cap conceals her hair, and is tied under her chin with white hemmed strings. She sports a gay bandanna gingham handkerchief folded neatly over her chest, and the ends crossed and pinned at the waist. Her feet are guiltless of the luxury of stockings, but look comfortable in stout carpet slippers. Her voice is equal in volume and strength to that of a strong man, and she shows none of the infirmities of age, except, perhaps, that she is not so clear-sighted as when she was a buxom young woman, when she saw the *wraiths of the last of the troubled spirits* of the sons of the forest.

As the sister of Aunt Patty is very deaf, our conversation is addressed to the latter, although we are told that Nancy has also a great fund of traditionary narrative.

The little log cabin has two comfortable rooms, and a half-story or garret loft above. The big outside stone chimney gives the structure a quaint look, and the same dimensions continued, for the fireplace within, is suggestive of the Yule log and a blazing fire.

But now the door stands wide open and from its threshold our eyes rest upon a mountain valley of Arcadian repose. Through this dreamy dell flows a rippling brook, and some quiet cows stand in the purling water, under the shadow of a clump of trees.

The old clock in the cabin strikes the mystic number three, recalling us from the reverie induced by the tranquil beauty of the landscape. So we go within. The rude home has a certain air of comfort: the single deal table, a few chairs, one old cupboard painted red, some treasured bits of delftware brought over from *dem Vaterlande* by the *Grossmutter*, a cracked blue teapot jauntily filling the foreground of the shelf, several cheap prints of gay contrasting red, blue, and green, the high bedstead with its full rounded feather beds on top, reaching midway to the low ceiling, and a glimpse of a Dutch-oven in the yard back of the cabin, all tell us at a glance that the ancestral tree planted here was German.

"Good morning, Aunt Patty; we have come to see you, and to hear all about the days when the Indians chased deer on this mountain."

"Cum in, cum in, Miss Green! Lord sakes! Ye'r very welcum! Haw, Haw, Haw! So ye want ter know all about the Injuns, do ye?" And her laugh was so awfully hearty it had a *roar* in it. "Yes, yes, yes!" rocking herself, "I jist can tell ye yarns, Injun yarns, tull ye say, enuf — raal Injun yarns. Why, Lord, woman! Down in Middle Creek Holler, the Injuns jist used to walk so constant like arter nite, they kep up a kinder *procession of shades!*"

"Aunt Patty, are any Indian ghosts ever seen or heard nowadays?"

"Why, no, woman; they'se no Injuns heerd now these gwine onter fifty yeers. Only the old folks knowed of 'em. But, Lord, woman! Whin we wuz children, we'd often's the time and agin walk one side to Middle Creek, an' *the Skiliton Injuns* jist friendly like, on t'other side, *hollerin'*; an' we wuz so used to it we didened skeer a bit. But now this many'se the yeer they's *laid.* I reckon *thar time's up!*"

"Aunt Patty, did you ever see these spooks?"

"Lord, yes, woman! Wonst thar wuz a huskin'. I wuz jist a young gal. We hed an orful supper, an' we wemen folks jined in ter cook it, an' we hed a roarin' time, I bet ye, woman. Wal, my brother, an' Cousin Adam, an' the one es wuz to be my old man, and sum more on us started toluble late at nite to go back. Now, we couldened turn off into the woods, bekas thar wuz a strait lane from the huskin', an' thin the road jist run along Middle Crick for a mile, an' thin we kim to a spot whar thar wuz a big rock like to a jumpin'-off place in the middle of the crick. Now, before hour road turned off anent the field, wal, we'd jist got to the ind like, whin Jake, he that wuz to be my old man, jist sawr a big lite, and lots of sparks off it. As we kim to the crick, we all sawr it was a big Injun shade *with a lite in him!* He wuz red from the waist up, and thin the rist of him wuz black. He wint strait along in the middle of the crick, an' we could see him plain *by the lite in him*, and the shower of sparks that wint up from him. He wint step by step, an' we heerd him in the stream, — splash, splash,— an' he hollered feerful, *Ok-en-jah!* Whin he kim to the big rock, he jist give one leap in the air, hollered *Ok-en-jah,* an' wint out in the water. Thin all was dark an' still. We wint quick over the field —"

"Aunt Patty, did you *really* see that?"

"Lord, yes, woman, an' morr too! My dad, as knowed the Injun lingo, he sed as *ok-en-jah* was like as ef you sed, good-bye. Why, Josh sed he wuz wonst jined by wun, an' he hed a fire in him; an' no hed to him, an' he skeered Josh's critter so, she wouldened git, but stud stock still; an' he hed to lead her along, she hed the trimbles so bad. This Injun was seed fifty times. They wuz seed in every kind of shape and form.

"Wunst, woman, when I wuz a lusty gal, I wint over a big clearin' to git the loan of a kittle for bilin' apple butter; an' es the folks over thar wus n't dun bilin' thar butter, I jist turned in an' holpt tull dark. Thin Dave told his nigger boy to holp me with the kittle, and so we wint acrosst the field. The stars wuz out shinin' but the moon wuz not up yit, an' jist es we wuz in the middle of the open field, whar wuz no trees, no brush, but a clearin' for plantin' corn, we seed a big black hoss sittin' upon his hunches, an' he hed his front feet hangin' limp like, — jist so! — es ef they wuz two hands, an' inside of his hed wuz big red eyes, rollin'. Lord, woman! That nigger boy wuz skeered that bad he sed, 'Miss Patty, I'd ruther be licked a hundred time than go whar that hoss is;' an' I sed, 'run on, you nigger, don't stop, don't look, hurry right on,' an' so we skeeted by. An' jist es we's got a bit away, the hoss hollered, *Ok-en-jah!* The nigger he kited back through the woods; an' the nixt day I looked all over that field, step by step, but nary a sign ef a hoss, or ef any critter, could I see — jist a big open, bare field. Yes, yes, woman they tuk on all shapes. I kin remimber well, wunst whin I was a stout chunk uf a gal, how skeered we allers wuz to go by the school-hus at night-time. Now, they *did* say that this school-hus wuz built on an Injun buryin'-ground; an' every night ef a body would pars that a way, thar it wuz to be seed, all lit up! One night, whin I wuz a little gal, en' hed bin with my dad acrosst that clearin' to go see a neighbor, an' the folks kep us tull arter dark, whin we wuz gwine back we hed to go jist by that school-hus, an' sure enuff thar wuz a big Injun with his *hed all on fire;* an' jist es we wuz edgin' off es fur es we could git, he hollered orful, and wint rite thro' an' thro' the school-hus door, en' we could hear inside like a trimblin' voice kumin' up from under the groon, *Ok-en-jah!*"

"Why, Aunt Patty, I should think the school-children

would have been afraid to go there?"

"Lord, no, woman! The Injuns wuz only seed and heered in the night-time. But I do remimber the orful time whin the school-mister kim near to bein' killt thar."

"Oh, Aunt Patty! How was that?"

"Haw! Haw! Haw! Woman. I wuz a-walkin' wunst in the eenin' with Jake, the wun es wuz to be my old man — it wuz in the time whin he wuz sparkin'. Now, we didened notis that we hed walkt right smart, untull we wuz, sure enuff, plum up by that school-hus; and thar wuz a lite in it! Now Jake, he wuz allers dare-devil like, and he sez, 'Patty, I'm bound to see what that ar lite means?" 'Oh, for the Lord's man, don't!' sez I; an' es he wud sort or make fur the door, I wud pull him back. So we kep furzin' fur a while. Thin we heerd a groan. 'Oh, Lord, Lord, man! Kim away — do!' sez I. 'The Injun's in thar, an' he'll cast spells on us. We'll be wizened.' 'But I will, Patty, an' thar's the ind on it,' shouted Jake, who throw'd hisself on the door, an' it flue open, an' thar, es I jist held on to his coat-tail — what didened we see, woman?"

"Oh, Aunt Patty! What? Don't stop there."

"Haw! Haw! Haw! Lord, woman, we seed the School-mistur! Thar he wuz, stiffund out like ded on the floor, an' the fire out, an' the room killin' cold, an' a candle burnin' on the Mistur's desk, an' all his books lyin' round; and he jist hed strength to say, 'I'm doubled in cramps, an' ef you want to save me, git me home.'"

"Now, in them days, the School-mistur boarded roun' a week at a time; and he wuz a boardin' at a hus right smart off. But me an' Jake, we tuk him hed an' heels, an' we toted him all the way. Me an' he wuz purty used up, whin we git him thar; but a roarin' fire an' hot whiskey an' plinty of it, an mustard an' blankits an' rubbin' settled him; and whin he kim to, he sed, — 'You two saved my life, with your sparkin.'" He sed he hed staid to set the ritin' copies fur the school, an' afore he know'd it the fire wint out, an' whin he would a gone, he hed a cramp. So that Injun fire wuz *his* taller candle — haw! Haw!"

"Well, Aunt Patty, that one, anyhow, was a good Indian?"

"Lord, yes, woman, you bet — but thar wuz Injun spooks, an' plenty of 'em. The folks do say that, seven or eight years gone by, they heered 'em tramp, tramp — splash, splash, up Middle Creek. But I reckon they'se *laid* now."

"Wunst — Lord, woman, how we did joke him! — Ike was walkin' near the crags, back of your hus, an' he'd bin to Andy's peach orchard; an' he had two hankies tied on a stick full of the peaches, which he hed tuk on the sly like — whin all on a suddint a big Injun shade with a lite in him run agin him that hard, he jist tottled over, an' that skeered, he split all his peaches.

"But, Lord, woman! It wuz no larfin' matter; fur ef you talked back — so much es one'word — they'd git riled and chase you.

"One night my gran-dad wuz walkin' along an' a big Injun *with a burnin' lite in him*, an' his hands all on fire, walked alongside of him in the middle of the stream, splash, splash! The sparks flew up above his hed, an' shot out frum his finger inds, an' he hooped an' hollered like mad; an' my gran-dad jist, careless like, morcked back. All to wunst the Injun broke away over the stream arter gran-dad, an' he got orful skeered an' run. An' the Injun chased him clean to his door; and es granny heerd him runnin' she opened the door quick fur him, an' he jist fell inside, an' the minit the door shet, the Injun hollered orful,
'Ok-en-jah!' — an'giv a thunderin' rap on the door, which sissed es ef a red-hot iron hed bin throw'd agin it, an' he lift the sign of his burnin' knuckles planted in the door, tull the house wuz tore down — an' meny hes seed the door.

"Lord, woman, why, my dad"—

"Aunt Patty, good-bye, and many thanks. Here is the making of a new dress for you, if you will take it; but I cannot stay to hear any more of these dreadful stories about 'Indian shades,' for if the dark overtakes me, as it will presently, I half believe some spook will chase me home too, with that horrible cry of — *Ok-en-jah! Good-bye.*"

Chapter IV

SUPERSTITIONS AND APPARITIONS

THE luminous phenomenon, commonly called Will-o-the-Wisp, or Jack-with-a-Lantern, is not unfrequently seen in the valleys at the foot of South Mountain, on either side of the mountain, or at times dancing with vaporous sheen along its slopes. Doubtless the recurrence of this *ignis fatuus* must impress the vulgar mind, that can only penetrate the surface of things, with a vague dread.

The deceptive phosphorescence, the visible atmosphere thus seen skipping about, has inspired awe, and the "Spook" has risen to confront the alarmed imagination. In fact, we find that the recitals in which the ghost figures are very numerous, and, what is more, accepted.

Descending the western slope, where the declivity is most romantic, and the National Road is cut in the side of the canyon, whose width is divided by a babbling brook for the entire distance, and the verdurous heights come down close upon you and form a leafy screen even in mid-day, — here, born of the blended influences, the Mystical finds its home.

Here the *Snarly Yow* and the *Werewolf* are believed to guard the pass; and presently we shall mention a few of the various instances, among many that are recounted, of the appearance of this formidable apparition, as well as others.

At times, indeed most frequently, of canine form and black in color, of a mystic shining; now waning, now increasing, it crosses the ravine, or disappears like a light suddenly blown out. Again, after night falls and spreads its pall of mystery over the canyon, the affrighted wayfarer beholds the *Phantom Soldier*, seated sadly silent beside the splashing stream, where it falls quite a depth under the bold, jutting rock.

In the night-gloom, or in the pallid early morning light, the lurid shimmer shows the Soldier Spook, stirring the camp fire and bent over its decaying embers, sullenly keeping his long vigil. Or mayhap the startled passer-by is overtaken by yet other noiseless foot-falls, that stalk beside him as he hurries on, pacing the boundary of another world.

Solemn, stately, grim, and gaunt are these shadowy Southern sentinels. They wearily wend their mournful march, until lost instantly to sight in the culvert of a bridge, only to reappear at some other time. The particular culvert under which these phantoms glide is pointed out.

We have been told that a spook of very awful mien and huge proportions has been seen, in the guise of a waggoner, to suddenly rise from the ground in the dell below South Mountain House, and lift his vast arms aloft. But no one has ever staid to see what else he did, or if he sank back into the same place from whence he came.

Being naturally very desirous to discover some explanation of these various appearances, we have tried to find out if there exist any decaying ligneous particles of an inflammatory nature, or if there are moist and marshy places, where gases are generated, that, upon being exposed to certain atmospheric conditions in the dark, would show some inflammation of carbonic fibres.

But we have gained no facts of any consequence explanatory of these shining vapors, except, indeed, the one fact that, under favorable circumstances, they may be and often are seen.

Although the current superstition about Friday is held in such inconvenient force that men refuse to commence work on that day, and also object to enter your service if a day is dark or cloudy, as being an unlucky omen; yet we have not been able to discover, except in the case of one "*doctress*," who performs cures by "spells," that the lunar phases, or the astral influences, are construed with reference to events that occur.

The South Mountain lunar orb may be semi-circular or horned, full and round, or only give a pale edge of opaline light, but there exists no Endymion upon these heights to read the meaning of degree or color.

The lunatics of South Mountain confess to no lunar over-mastering power. The prognostics here derived are a grosser sort, have no lucid specks, and would seem to be of more defined diabolic shape.

In speaking of various narratives of South Mountain apparitions, we will first notice the statements regarding the "*Black Dog*," as the mountaineers call it.

What is quite remarkable regarding this delusion, if such it is, is that the spectre of the Dog-Fiend has appeared to so many people, who aver to have seen it, and that, from their descriptions, it has invariably been noticed very near the same place.

The different accounts all agree in the main points, and are difficult to dispose of by a mere denial, or by the charge of hallucination, which may more readily perhaps be made than sustained. This canine marvel has so often been stated to have appeared, that some persons consider repetition of this appearance as a proof that some singular occurrence is repeated in that locality. Yet these matter-of-fact people, who have not investigated, but relied exclusively on their own preconceived ideas of the probable, have been unwilling to suppose that there could exist any element of the unreal in this matter other than the excited imaginations of the mountaineers. They have therefore supposed it to be some wild animal whose *habitat* has never been properly explored, and that infests the same spot, always taking the same paths after nightfall.

Then others again, equally intelligent, and perhaps more inquiring, deem that this view of the case is quite inadmissable, because no visible traces have ever been found indicating the actuality of a savage beast. If indeed such an animal ranged the forest, it would at least occasionally commit depredations, and it would also be more likely to frequent more remote and even inaccessible places, and not haunt an open forest path, or cross the National Road at a point so generally traveled over, so accessible to pursuit, and where it would most likely be caught or killed before any length of time had transpired.

While others, again, suppose it to be some animal who stalks from its lair at night to slake its thirst at the wayside spring; where it has been asserted that it was seen. In all the narratives concerning this vision that we have heard, substantially the same course is mentioned. The Black Dog comes down a certain narrow and darksome path, crosses the road where it intersects this path, descends the hill on the same continuous path, crosses the stream, and is soon lost to sight as it ascends the opposite height of the canyon. Now, this course, marked out for its wanderings, is very near inhabited places.

Commanding the view of the immediate entrance of this mysterious cleft in the mountain is a restful summer home, aptly called Glendale. It comprises about twenty acres of such pleasing and diversified scenery as one rarely meets in so small compass. Back of the home the ground rises abruptly to a point called the Pinnacle, which is thickly covered with forest trees, while the base of the hill is beautified by a fine fruit orchard, whose profuse bloom fills the air with fragrance. Not far from the tempting orchard, a sinuous path leads us into the little garden, with its look of comfort, from whence we walk under the grateful shade of a grape-vine arbor to the simple home. Meandering through the grounds farther on, is the mountain brook, whose serpentine course enriches a smiling meadow, then coyly hides and murmurs in mossy bed as it courses onward under a mass of overhanging wild vines, then emerging into broader view, allows itself to be utilized as it runs through what is called the Spring House. As we enter this little stone structure built over the water, we are at once refreshed by the cool ripple of the wavelets circling round the crocks of delicious creamy milk that stand in rows. But soon we leave the cheering shelter to pursue with more rapid step the now willful onward progress of the stream, that, all too quickly and with tumultuous haste, makes its unchecked exit into the awesome gorge. And here, almost on the verge of Glendale, the Black Dog eludes the eager vision.

Now once more we pause, and on the threshold give wistful gaze back to the rural home. The white geese and more sober-liveried ducks disport themselves in the water, while the careful hen and chickens look on with a comical air of wise reproof, then, scratching busily, catch the poor little grub-worm, who would fain live out its summer day unharmed. The naughty, pretty, white goat browses on the hillside, the patient cows "chew the cud" in the clover field, the droning bee hums in the locust-tree, and the merry children are at play on the sward; while best of all, the loving mother, seated on the rustic bench, carols out of her heart full of joy the sweetest natural notes, whose rich music dies away on the balmy air, only to float with echo fainter still into the mystic space beyond. We feel like one standing on the confines of two worlds. The rural home gives us warmth and light, and we must perforce wait until the last gorgeous rays of the declining sun have faded into dim crepuscular shade, and the gray twilight into sombre night, before bidding adieu to Glendale. We gain the perilous path of the "Snarly Yow" —

Our first narrator, and a credible witness, is William L—e. He is a good type of a sturdy mountain man. A sober, laborious, strong, and trustworthy young man, of perhaps thirty years of age. He is married, and lives with his little family in the first cabin on the brow of the hill that overlooks Glendale. His hut is not over a quarter of a mile from the alleged habitat of the Black Dog.

One night about ten o'clock, as he was returning from the village of Boonsboro', whither he had gone to make some little purchases for his family, he encountered the Black Dog. It was clear starlight, and the ungainly form of the beast could be distinctly traced. It was black, and bigger than any dog he had ever seen; and, as he came nearer, the object intercepted him, and stood guarding the road in such a way as to forbid his crossing. So, to use his own expression, he *"fit him."* That is, nothing daunted, he fought at him. But, to his confusion, as the creature was attacked, it *"grew longer,"* and presently seemed to extend across the road, making no noise, but showing a very wide and very ugly-looking red mouth; while, all the time the thick and heavy blows rained down upon it, the sinewy arm of the woodsman met with no resistance, but rather seemed to beat the air.

Presently the still lengthening shadow passed onward, and then the man, not a little flurried at the strange nature of the vision, went home; nor did he receive the least bodily harm from this ominous combat.

But we have several times heard him tell this story when questioned about it, and when one looks upon the erect and well-knit figure of this "stalwart tiller of the soil," and his firm and composed bearing, one cannot but wonder how such a man could have had a spectral illusion.

A farmer relates, that passing along the "Gorge" at night he saw the Black Dog stalking down the hillside path, and as he stopped to look at him he had the sensation *"that the hill* was coming down upon him," which almost paralyzed his faculties, so benumbed did he feel

45

— "My nervous system was racked to the centre," the man said, in telling his story! Of course, every one knows, when *a man's nerves* are shaken, that it means something very dreadful, and not at all like the "nervous spasms" that foolish women fall into for just nothing at all; and it certainly never means that a man is at all frightened . . .

Another man, who can see farther than most other men, once saw the mythical dog beyond its usual route, and coming out of a tumble-down old stable higher up on the road. This man was seized with a sort of "color blindness," as the vision assumed various hues, at times "coal black," then again changing into great spots of white. . . . .

A Mr. P—r, who is an itinerant preacher, avers to have seen it I am told, at three different times, when, after holding evening prayer-meeting in the little whitewashed church beyond Glendale, he was passing the fabulous spot on his return home. We are not informed whether the myth was pommelled with orthodox blows, or dismissed with an Avaunt, Satan. . . . Also, Mr. A—y M—e saw it once. . . . Mr. W—y, who is considered "a sure shot," relates to have met it crossing the road. He carried his ever-ready rifle with him, and feeling sure of his aim, shot at it with steady hand when within a few paces. To his speechless amazement, the well-directed shot went right through the animal without effect. Again and again the sharp crack of the trusted rifle was heard, as it was sent with deadly accuracy, and went whizzing through and through the shadow, leaving no mark. Overcome with dread at the uncanny sight, the huntsman fled, nor stopped to see if the shade retreated or pursued. A mountain man, who is so large of stature that he is called "Big Joe," told us, that once, being on horseback, he saw the Black Dog suddenly start up from the road and run on before his horse, and that as it ran the creature threw up dirt and gravel in its tracks, very much as any clumsy beast with claws might do when in a rapid run. That he chased it, but utterly failed to overtake it, when it disappeared as mysteriously as it had appeared. Now Big Joe is very fond of a joke, and not a few "good ones" has he "played off" in this very gorge, which he tells in a sly and confidential way, jokes that were no jokes to the terrified victims, who to this day are ready to swear under oath to the wonderful things they saw. He told us once, with a quiet chuckle, that he had wrapped straw tightly round the rim and spokes of an old wagon-wheel, when watching his opportunity as a timid neighbor was coming up the Gorge one night, he set fire to this wheel and sent it whirling down the road in its erratic course. The fiery circle thus rapidly descending, caused a great panic, and the poor belated farmer in spite of his dread of a shrewish reception from an irate wife, rushed back to the village, declaring he would not trust himself in the Gorge till morning.

Now, although Joe looked very solemn when he told us of this adventure with the dog, we are not quite certain after all, whether the "horse," the "Black Dog," "the claws," the "dirt and gravel," in a word, the very chase itself, may not have been an invention. We, personally, vouch for nothing, except the telling of our stories.

A man, who has always lived on the Mountain, states that he saw the Black Dog in the Gorge, just below the spring, and threw a cane at it, which seemed not to hit it, but to go through it.

The wife of a farmer who lives on the summit beyond South Mountain House, and who is a woman of physical strength and nerve, as well as of very good judgment and what is called common sense, told us that, coming up the Gorge one night with her husband in a sleigh, the moon being well up and the night bright, she distinctly saw the animal standing near the spring; that it was of much larger size than any dog she had ever seen, but looked, as it stood against the snowy bank, brown in color; that, as they approached it, the horse snorted, and was so restive as to demand all her husband's attention, and that she was afraid to point it out to him, as she knew, from his fearless character, that he would insist upon stopping to attack it. As they passed on, with the instinct that women have inherited from Lot's wife, she looked back, and there it stood, just as she had first seen it. . . .

There is a current belief that this apparition is more often seen by animals than by man, and that when horses stop at this spot at night, and tremblingly refuse to move, one must pause and not foolishly press them forward, for the Black Dog fills the path, and one must wait its passage; as it is considered rash and reckless to try and urge a horse against the Dog-Fiend.

. . . We know a mountain farmer who is a man of remarkable size and has great strength. So strong is he, that it is related of him that, on one occasion when visiting a near village, he became so hilarious and noisy that the attempt was made to arrest him and shut him up over night in what is called "the Jug." The man, Samson-like, successfully routed the constabulary force of the village, then, doubtless sobered by the effort, quietly mounted his horse and rode home. Now, whether our narrative dates back to this ride, or refers to some other occasion, when perhaps he was under equally high pressure, we know not, but it is related that, riding up the Gorge one night, to his great wrath, the Black Dog stopped the way. With many a blow and added curse he tried to spur his frightened horse past the obstruction, until poor Equinus, goaded past all endurance, became mad with mingled rage and terror, and threw his master to the ground, breaking his collar-bone in the fall.

We have selected the foregoing instances, among others, because we personally know all these people, and we believe that they would not readily be daunted by meeting any object, however terrifying in aspect, if they could have accounted for the vision as being in the natural order of things. These mountaineers are made hardy by the life of exposure they are forced to lead; and they are used from childhood to the terrible winter storms that rage with wild fury on their mountain top.

As for ourselves, our province is to narrate the circumstances attending this spectral apparition, be it illusive, delusive, or of real purport, *as they have been told to us.*

Certainly a number of persons have met the vision, and their accounts do not materially vary. Actually, they substantially agree.

We cannot refuse to receive the evidence of trustworthy witnesses, nor have we as yet heard any hypothesis given on this subject, of satisfactory explanation.

Thus we leave the Werewolf, the Snarly Yow, the Dog-Fiend, the Black Dog, in possession of this romantic canyon. To us he is a delightful but harmless creation, and we would not willingly "lay" his Ghostship.

We love in the shades of evening, as we drive past the obscure woods he ranges, to salute him as the dauntless Cerberus of this historic Thermopylae; where, doing faithful duty, he ever guards from intrusion the nodding shades of sentinels beyond.

The fanciful Celtic superstitions are all unknown to South Mountain, and on her mossy banks or amid her lonesome dells are never found the airy imprint of the Queen of Elfland, nor the magic rings of the moonlit sward, left by the blithesome revelry of the dance. One looks in vain deep in her forest depths for trace of fay or fairy.

Yet more beautiful than fairy-land is the embowered path, all redolent with the sweet perfume of the wild grape, or the delicate aroma of the wild rose.

And oft in the dewy morn the poet, seeking her canopied recesses, finds the tear of the Peri in the meek eye of the hidden violet, or with shuddering glimpse meets the evil glance of the morose Gnome peering from out the gloomy bowers of her laurel thicket. Again the imagination catches the dark shadow of the savage Brown Man of the Moors in her waste places, while her encircling rocks, like weeping Niobes, bend their craggy heads and through every mystic crevice, sigh and moan.

Yet, except in the wild reverie of fancy, she has not risen to the ethereal inspiration of an Ariel, nor can mortal ear hear, mingling with the glad song of the mountain rill, the plaintive but melodious chant of the White Lady of Avenel.

These are the realms of fancy which she aspires not to invade. . . . But, for all that, South Mountain has a sort of Banshee, an apparition of more homely kind, spoken of as the "White Woman."

The appearance of this figure is dreaded, because supposed to announce a death in the family, or at least, if not actually fraught with swift-coming disaster, to bode no good. As an example, it was told us that a mother died, leaving a baby nine days old in the charge of the grandmother. Two days after the death of the mother, the granny saw her daughter's wraith come back and lean over her baby's cradle. She then knew that the baby must go too; and in effect the little one only survived two weeks after that. Only in one other instance narrated to us was it asserted that the Banshee was the actual harbinger of death in the family. But, of course, these one or two cases are quite enough to arouse a superstitious dread of this visitant.

The log cabin stood very near the National Road. A flourishing grape-vine, supported by some rudely cut poles, gave grace to the doorway, while a cluster of gay sunflowers lent an unconscious aesthetic air, and relieved the uncomfortable look of the family pig wallowing in his extemporized mud-hole, beside the tumble-down picket fence.

An old woman, her son, and her grand-daughter Annie lived in this hut. Now, Annie is a simple mountain girl, with no knowledge outside of the narrow confines of the life she leads; and to see her, any one would say that, except, perhaps from an indigestion, she could not have an optical illusion. Yet on this still summer eve, as she sat in the doorway, looking vacantly out upon the road only a few feet distant, there suddenly uprose from its hard and flinty surface the shrouded figure of the White

Woman. With a piercing shriek Annie swooned away, and on coming to her senses, she told the granny that the apparition had approached her, and seemed to pass on into the house. Two days later Ike, the grown son of the old woman, died. It would be quite useless to try and dispossess the minds of these people of the firm belief that the White Woman came to announce this death, or was not in some uncanny way responsible for this calamity. Here we have the veritable Banshee predictive of death. And to add to the terror, the hut, not long after this occurrence, took fire, and now lies in shapeless ruin.

A young lad avers to have seen the White Woman at the wayside spring in the Gorge, where the Black Dog is so often met. Inasmuch as this boy is only half-witted, we mention this story, to show how strong is the general belief in this phantom, when his recital is noticed and credited.

Another person, who certainly cannot be accused of a vivid imagination, has seen her walking in the glen with a handkerchief tied around her head. Not a very romantic phantom!!

Indeed, at times it requires but very little to frighten people who are disposed to be credulous. For instance, a woman told us, as a secret and a good joke, that she had adopted a contrivance to drive away from around her cabin in the evening some noisy boys, who repeatedly kept her awake until a later hour than she liked.

She said that, being no longer able to endure the disturbance, she had risen from her bed one night, and, wrapping a white blanket around her, which she held slightly raised above her head, she marched forth thus equipped before the bewildered gaze of the noisy youngsters. As she had supposed would be the case, they did not stop to catch more than a momentary glimpse of the white figure, when, shouting altogether, "the White Woman! The White Woman!" they trooped off in a hurry; and a subdued quiet reigned that night in Zittlestown. This is one of our *secrets*, which we tell in strict confidence to our "dear public."

But, if you were to tell this practical joke to every mother's son of the neighborhood, they would answer that, for all that, for sure and certain, the White Woman did appear.

Now, for an example. Dave's wife really did see the White Woman, and for all we know, some harm may yet come of it, even if it is years and years afterwards.

Well, Dave's wife was walking along that long, lonely lane on the top of the hill one evening, making her way home with her little child of four years as fast as she could, as they were belated, when the child, pulling at its mother's gown, cried out, "Look, muz!" She looked, and was much alarmed to see the White Woman. Fortunately, almost at the moment, the spook vanished. Now, here we have the raw material for some future scribe to indite a walking Erl-king of South Mountain; the child grasping fast for protection to the sheltering embrace of the mother.

Henry tells us that he has seen the White Woman in the Gorge, but that he hurried on. He now greatly regrets that he did not stop and investigate. Yet we venture to opine, for all that, he will be likely, upon a repetition of the same apparition, to do just the same thing; that is, hurry onward.

Otho H—l, we are told, has been greatly troubled by
the frequent appearance of the phantom at his bedside;
and the neighbors shake their heads, and say it has a bad
effect upon his mind, as he seems to be growing very
low-spirited. From all of which it will be seen that the
White Woman can neither be confronted by primer or
prayer-book, for she is an accepted fact.

Although the appearance of this spook is viewed with
dread, yet she is mild and pleasant of aspect, compared
with some others that we wot of.

There is a grewsome spectre that, during the
penitential advent time preceding Christmas, is seen,
until happily it is "laid" for that year by the recurrence
of the holy festival.

In these dreary, bitter cold December nights, this
awful phantom it is said, emerges from a dense forest half
a mile distant and eastward of South Mountain House.
Darkling, headless, and dragging in fleshless grasp a
clanging chain, it may be heard slowly advancing! Sere
crackle the countless leaves that, stark and stiff, lie
prone o'er the grave of the too short summer joys.

How they shrivel under the *presence*, while the
responding crystal springs they once have sheltered,
convulsive sigh, bound by their icy cerements, more
closely binding and condensing still, as the drear
phantom makes its solemn round.

The merciful snow has covered the bald and jutting
rocks, and hidden away the lovely ferns and graceful
maiden-hair nestling close in their sinuous crevices.
Yet these tiny stems blacken with fear as the encrusted
breath floats by. But when the vernal breath of spring
shall renew their vigor, again they will give forth the
aroma of a resuscitated life, expanding into the tropic

vision of their mimic palm-leaf beauty. The huge skeleton forms of the forest trees stand statuesque witnesses, as the solemn shade progresses, baring their bony arms and bending their gnarled and distorted limbs under the weight of winter's relentless grasp.

And now we hear the clangor of the chain, crisp, rattling o'er the frozen surface of the meadow streamlet, until presently the gaunt and headless phantom gains the broad belt of the National Road, and ever wrapped in gloom, passes South Mountain House, disappearing with resounding echo amid the battle-crags beyond.

This, it is said, is the solemn expiation a tormented soul has been doomed to undergo for the past fifty years, whose mortal offence was a dishonest act. There was a dispute with a neighbor about the land down in the meadow, which the too thrifty farmer settled one night in his own favor by moving the stone landmarks. Then the next day, dragging a surveyor's chain over the place, he made the boundary line to suit himself. Nor did the land-owner suspect the fraud. Alackaday! if such and so great is the heavy penance inflicted for *one* grasping act, may we not fear to see, some cold December night in yon crowded city, where the starving Lazarus has been driven with contumely from the door of the modern Dives, and the hour of Dive's doom shall come, that then his tormented shade shall groan under the pitiless weight of whole rows of brown-stone houses built by dishonest gains, — gains wrested from the nefarious moving of the landmarks of that golden rule, which hedges in and sacredly defines "mine and thine." Yet doubtless in these cases the damnation is too deep for mortal eye to scan, and the load so heavy that the sinner is sunk forever and forever out of sight. Amen.

On account of our being so very tender-hearted and sensitive, it has given us great pain to have to chronicle the last dreadful story; but with us fidelity to duty reigns paramount, and we have promised our readers a truthful narrative. We are, therefore, all the more pleased that it now becomes our province to relate a more successful sortie.

We like to use French words wherever it is permitted, to turn aside the Saxon force with a mild and fine point!

Mais revenons a nos revenants! Which means, let us return to our spooks.

It is indeed pleasant to be able to say, that one very distressing case is supposed to be "laid," and the ghost now happily at rest after his cold vigils and long wanderings.

But we must not, because we are cheerful, let "our right hand forget its cunning," and anticipate.

It all happened in this wise. Grandfather Q— was flatly accused of moving a corner-stone to suit his own purposes. The old man had been much worried by his next neighbor whose land was "jinin' on," too close to suit perfect convenience. According to our informant, they two had had "much scribblin an furzin one with t'other," which, we understand, is local parlance for lawyers' contentions about straightening out the line of boundary. Wearied out probably by the length of this legal operation, farmer Q— decided to adjust the corner-stone to suit himself. Calling upon his stalwart son to help him one night, the whole business that was consuming so much needless red tape was very speedily settled, so these short-sighted men thought at the time; but unhappily for them, the end was not yet. For just as the two, father and son, had thought to be quite comfortable, after all the "lawin'" —the old man without being given any time to repent, —died. But, for all that, he did not exactly "give up the ghost," for while his mortal body was still unburied, his spirit came back to his house, and looked in on his son, who was just about (as so many thousands of sons and heirs-at-law before him had done) to enter into peaceable possession of the ill-gotten gains.

Now, this very vicious ghost "looked in on him," and bade his "said" son and heir to "come on." These were the very words this uncivil spook used.

Then this obedient son went back to his own inner room, and so terribly had the ghost of his cruel old father frightened him, that his knees knocked together, he fell into a shivering fit, had a spasm of the heart — and died — died before sundown of that very day. Nor are we told that other expiation happened *to him*, than the giving up his life as a penalty for his part in the sin.

But farmer Q— fared not so well; for, not content with having ousted his lawful heir, this abominable spook would walk the open fields — coming down where what is called the "county road" joins the "pike," — all the while lugging in a fiery hand a red-hot stone, being the identical one he had cheated with, barring the heating.

Well, this uncomfortable state of things for the country at large went on for a long time, until everybody declared him to be a first-class fraud and nuisance.

Yet, whenever anybody would meet this fiery sinner, one would naturally give him the road, and get out of the way; so that he never had any opportunity to make known that the "spell" could be broken, and he, miserable rover, "laid."

Now, after many a year of public penance, "his time" doubtless being up, and above all, the good Lord so willing it, the spook met on the county road one night a rollicking young fellow, who, nothing daunted by the shower of sparks that flew from him, mocked at him, and called out, in allusion to the hot stone the spook carried, "Where shall I put it?" This was, indeed, a very sarcastic hit at the fact that he had for so many years been compelled to hold that stone, and never been able to rest for one moment by putting it down. Indeed, had the young fellow received a classical education, he would probably have called out, "Avaunt, old Susyphus!" and passed on, as every one else had done. But, fortunately for the spook, this merry braggart was guiltless of the Ancients; and so the blessed, blessed time the tortured phantom had so longed for had come. With hollow and sepulchral voice the phantom echoed back, "Where shall I put it?" To which the impudent youngster forthwith replied, "Fool, *put it where you got it.*" Thank Heaven, this injunction did the work, and that ghost was "laid;" for it went straight to the place where the landmark had been changed, and put that stone — suddenly grown cold — where he got it from. The moral that this country spook teaches, is *the necessity of restitution,* for it was assured to us, as a certain and awful fact, that this spook would have been a public pest till Doomsday, unless he had made the crooked line straight. And we all know like gospel truth without any one telling us, — that of course this spook had to have this help. Now, in this world restitution comes so very easy, after all; for it only depends on ourselves and our own free will to effect the right, and do the fair and square thing: while we see plainly enough by this story, and many other things that we know of, that, in the next world, we can do nothing for ourselves, but have to depend on the good will of others in our regard. The old woman who was so obliging as to narrate to us this instructive story (although the moral reflections are ours, not hers), also told us that "it was a sure thing" that when ghosts came back they were "not in a good place." Because, she says, "if they are in a good place, they stay where they are." This opinion, be it understood, is not dogma, but only her individual private judgment.

While we are clanking our chains, be it known that some persons quietly hint that still another venerable sinner, who moved a landmark, has been seen in the shape of a black dog, dragging a chain, and that this agreeable new phase has already taken a clearly marked route, being seen and heard in that direction where the offence was committed. In view of the frequency of this kind of punishment, we would philanthropically advise all land speculators to beware of Old South Mountain, because if they overreach in their bargains on its summit, although they may go scot-free in this world, they will be sure to have a hard time of it hereafter. Nor would they like it, to become an example, a terror, or a laughing-stock to the descendants of those whom they have treated unkindly.

Yet that absolute truth that we worship, compels us to add that we have some fear that this last wraith is a dark and malicious exaggeration, hinting towards some old family feuds; the only authenticated Black Dog being the one that guards the canyon. Still, other shades appear, although the instances, so far as we have learned of their particular appearance, are isolated, and not given with that cumulative testimony that attests the "Black Dog," the "White Woman," and the "Headless Man." These are the trio of dreaded shades.

One moonlight night, a merry party of four, which everybody who knows anything also knows means two and two; walked out in the direction of the battle-field. As they reached the ground where in fiercest opposition men had once rushed to deadly combat, they became greatly alarmed at the distinct sound of *rattling sabres under the earth*, — sounds issuing from whence never more may mortals sabres clank.

They hurried away from the mysterious spot.

. . . Of course, it would be very unpoetical to suggest that they may have heard the jarring noise of the rattle-snake disturbed in his den. Nor do we venture such a practical view, only to make the remark that, under similar circumstances, it would be more dreadful to us to hear the warning note of this awful reptile, than an indefinite number of buried rusty sabres. Indeed, we surmise that it may have been both the one and the other!

. . . Another wonderful adventure was narrated to us. An old woman was walking along the road, with several other persons, when she saw suddenly arise from the ground a man on horseback, "a charging steed careering fast," whom no one else could see. This horse and rider, we are assured, must undoubtedly have been phantoms, because their appearance was sudden and noiseless, and they vanished almost as quickly as they appeared. Just, for instance, as if one was to see a shadow momentarily projected. It will be understood that we only use this comparison to elucidate.

Apropos of seeing sights, Mrs. H—l informs us that upon two occasions she saw a mysterious light moving along the road! She has no theory on the subject, which is more wonderful still!!!

This same old lady also makes known to us a very surprising meteorological phenomenon, which seems altogether to have escaped the scientific attention of our savants of the Weather Bureau. And this in face of the fact that the Government employs them to do it a signal service, and they have every advantage accruing from the combined operations of wind and weather, charts, all accurately mapped out. Besides this, the country furnishes all contrivances to weigh the air, so as to find out its state of dryness or its moisture, as well as no end of the most improved patents of thermometers, barometers, hygrometers, and anemometers.

Yet, to the glory of woman and her work be it said that one unassisted old woman on the top of South Mountain has made an observation of more real import to moral science, to the physical laws that govern the universe, and to society in general, than any scientific system of charts has developed. These charts may indicate disturbances, but her observation gives the cause. And it is this, *"When one, walking out of a cold winter's night, suddenly meets a warm current of air,* IT IS THE DEVIL!"

We were told that Samuel H—l noticed a light at the stone wall, not far from his house. When he tried to get across the ditch by the side of the wall, in order to examine and ascertain the cause of the light or its nature, he found to his astonishment that some invisible force held him back so that he could not cross this place, usually of easy access to him. This curious conceit reminds us of the mythical stories of the magic flames the Druids caused to appear, in order to keep back profane eyes from sacred rites.

There is a certain spring in the Gorge which is walled in, and at the outlet nearly even with the road, where the weary and heated pedestrians lie down on the ground, and "lap up" the water with their parched tongues. It is asserted that at such times a dog lies down beside them and "laps the water" also.

Perhaps, indeed, this phantom dog might be resolved into an airy echo within the walls of this spring. For we opine that, when a man laps water with his tongue, and prostrate on the ground, the echo of his action would sound strikingly like that of a dog, under the same circumstances, doing the same thing. We do not mean to disturb any belief in the nymph of this spring, or the mystical influence prevailing; for indeed we absolutely know nothing about it. Yet, such influences, we are constantly assured, exist there. A man told us that at this very spring, where shadowy sounds disport and lap the air, he "saw a shade," which as instantly vanished without taking a single "lap" at the spring.

And near this spot a farmer, walking down the valley past Glendale, onward into the heart of the glen that lies cradled beyond, saw a form walking steadily on before him. Feeling lonely, he called out to the person to stop, and he would "go along with him and keep him company." But the figure paid no attention to his request. However, upon being again addressed, the form suddenly turned around, when the farmer to his dismay, knew it to be *the spook* of an old neighbor who had died not long before. But fortunately it did not join him as requested, for a friendly chat, but was so obligating as to instantly vanish. In the presence of all these perplexing wonders, we stand confused at the closed portals of science, and cry out, "Open sesame!"

It is also of current belief that the happy mortals who are born in the sacred time between Christmas and New Year's Day have "the second sight," and can "see sights" invisible to less fortunate eyes.

Now, although we can well understand that it really is a great privilege to come into this mundane sphere, while the angels are rejoicing with renewed acclaim, during the octave of Christmas, yet we are naturally too timid to be among those who would appreciate it as a boon to be able to "see sights," *id est* ghosts of black dogs, white women, and headless men. The fact is, one ought to go through this wicked world anyhow, with their eyes introverted and muttering prayers. It is safer, therefore, to have one's range of vision rather restricted than enlarged. Finally, we know we shall open our eyes, forever (if we have made good use of them in this world) into a better world in the next. When Democritus put out his own eyes, in order that his intellectual life might not be disturbed, it was after having seen the world and studied it carefully through extensive travel, preferring the domain of the mind to any other possible range of vision. Evidently he was not a *seer.*

Chapter V

HAUNTS AND EIDOLON

THE prevalence of such a confused mass of superstition as we chronicle, within fifty miles of the very
capitol of this vast nation, and notwithstanding the
existence of the little public school-house and the little
whitewashed meeting-house beside it, in the very heart
of the mountain valley, does not prove much as regards a
theory of progressive civilization, and the wonderful
enlightenment of the nineteenth century. The truth is,
that this vaunted progress really cannot be said to exist,
except, perhaps, in the domain of the mechanical arts.
Of course, when we make such an assertion we know
that, in order to properly support a thesis of this nature,
that a volume of indefinite size might be written. There
is no study, probably, more useful to give the mind
something like a just balance, than the comparison of
the various forms of civilization, ancient and modern.
And yet when such comparisons are made, as they often
are, from a sophistical standpoint, they do more harm
than good. The class of minds that stultify this present
era, without looking carefully through the long vista of
the past ages, very much resemble those people who,
staying closely at home, make their own contracted
notions the standard of excellence.

The present age passes by St. Simon of Stylites poised
on his pillar, and jibes at him as an undoubted madman,
quite unconscious all the while that he has gained a
wider range of vision from his serene height of

contemplation, than the dust-stained pilgrims who revile him as they plod onward in the highway below.

If we glance at the many forms of superstition that have prevailed in the various ages and countries of the world, we will find that the practices and superstitions fostered, as it were, almost under the shadow of the grand Dome of Liberty, are rather of the lower than the higher forms.

Nor is this to be wondered at, for it is in very fact the outcome of our material civilization, where the making of money, the uses of money, and, too often, the mere sordid hoarding of money, count first. While the sensual in life, and the sensuous in the arts and literature, and no God as primal cause in science, have taken the place of the ideal aspirations of faith.

Now, there are superstitions which, although they arise as a result of intellectual ignorance, are nevertheless the index of purity of heart, and are rather untutored manifestations of an upspringing desire of the soul to reach the Unseen. Of these may be classed the lovely legends clinging on to the ardent faith of the so-called "dark ages," although not received as of faith.

These accepted legends and traditions, orally handed down from generation to generation, frame in the life of the lowly peasant who believes in them, with the absolute beauty of the brilliantly illuminated border of the quaint manuscripts of that age. These borders enclosed, perhaps, a black lettering, but they expressed the true.

As we write, a vision as of another and a better world comes before us. We behold the majestic, solemn repose of the monastery, and standing in a niche, as it were, set apart, a venerable figure, with bared head bowed down over the sacred desk in profound contemplation. For here is the Holy Bible, fondly clasped, with its *protecting* chain. The reader, in attitude of deepest reverence, ponders over the words of inspiration, while the pure heart rises to God in loving response to His word.

Angels pause in their swift course, as with radiant

wings they traverse illimitable space, and flash the reflected light and halo of benediction from the Uncreated Throne upon the scene. And Art, enkindling in her rapt musings, catches the light and the halo as it falls. And, in this same spirit, every household should erect for the Word of God a family altar, where this sacred volume should be held with awe. Such faith was of the past. Now what *is* of the present?

It is a long pilgrimage, to be sure, from the mediæval ages to the present day, and our sandals are turned into shoes, and our shoes have lost their soles in the toilsome journey. So we are at last here, in the broad light of progress, and we enter a fashionable shop to get others more suited to the advanced ideas around us. We are duly pinched and excruciated, somewhat as we once saw the martyrs tortured, only now there is no motive in our suffering to ennoble it; and finally we are told we have "a fit." How we sigh for the graceful old sandals, that we wore loosely strapped, without having "a fit," and not high-stepping, tight-compressing, all-torturing, with thin understanding, iron heels and steel springs as are these. But we are assured that our purchase is of the most improved patent and latest style, and our package is handed us.

As we stretch forth our hands to receive it, what blur or film fills our eyes, once so bright with visions of the glorious past? Can we longer see, or do we dream? — for the shoes handed us are wrapped in the rudely torn leaves of *a Bible!* "May God forgive the impiety!"[1] we exclaim. "The Bible," answers the flippant salesman, "is of no special value; it is spread broadcast in this nine-teenth century, not chained to the desk as in the Dark Ages. It is cheaper to us than other waste paper, for it is given away by thousands."

[1]This incident was narrated to us as of actual occurrence in Washington.

Among the pagan superstitions of South Mountain is found the belief in the *Taisch* or "Double." These visions as repeated to us, resemble the *Simulacra* of the ancient Romans.

The wraith called the "Double," is in effect a dual image of one's self or of another person still living, which, when it appears, is supposed to be predictive of the near-coming death of the person whose shadow is thus projected from out that spirit land he is so soon destined finally to enter.

In other words, the appearance of the *Taisch* is regarded as a premonition of death. . .

Henry C., a respectable man, told us that, when a boy of ten years of age, he saw one of these visionary likenesses, —the *Doppelganger* of the Germans.

He shared the same bed with his father's brother, Christopher, and one day he awoke and saw in the early gray of the morning, standing near the bed, a figure whom he supposed to be his uncle. But at the same moment, also noticing that his uncle was beside him in bed, he became greatly frightened. Christopher then spoke to his little nephew very calmly, telling him not to be afraid, and as he spoke the shadow vanished. The man then rose, dressed himself, and went down-stairs, where meeting Henry's father, he said to him, "Brother, *my double* has come for me, and Henry also has seen it. I shall not be with you long in this world."

After that he grew melancholy, could eat nothing, and lost strength, day by day. Being an old man, he did not long survive this enervation, and two weeks later died.

Apropos of this dual vision, a man told us a very curious story of a ghost and its double. It seems that his father's house was very near a graveyard, and the children of the family had, on account of its vicinage, lost all sense of awe as connected with the graves.

They found it quite convenient to join several other children who lived not far off, and towards evening have a game of hide-and-seek among the tombstones.

They never troubled themselves with stories of

corpse-candles, wraiths, or any of the uncanny traditions of burial-places; but right merrily raced about, crouching down, jumping up, and shouting in mad delight when the hot chase resulted in capture. Now there was living in the same neighborhood a big boy, who, having observed these children at play, conceived the idea of giving them a fright.

So one evening, enshrouding himself very carefully in white, he crouched behind a sheltering tombstone, where he waited until the children came very near where he was. Then suddenly he rushed forth from his place of concealment in pursuit. They all ran shrieking, "A spook! A spook! "as fast as possible, scrambling over the wall as best they could, and making their escape. One youngster however, stumbled, and, looking back, shrieked "There are two of them!" This outcry caused the youth who was playing off the trick on the poor frightened children to look back. To his utter constern-ation there was what seemed to be a veritable ghost — pursuing *him*!

Tearing off all disguise, that he might fly unincum-bered, and with fearful yells of terror, he rushed from that graveyard, the most affrighted of the troop.

"None of us," added the man, "ever cared to play among those tombstones again, for we were all quite sure that the second one was a *real ghost.*"

This narrative, which was told us in a very grave way, shows the influence of certain localities, on account of the associations connected with the places themselves, to prepare the mind for the mysterious or the dreadful, as well as to assist to enkindle the imagination by the faintest analogies, or perchance the loosest resemblances, to some other object which the excited fancy may call forth. . . .

A countryman told us of an adventure that he had of a similar sort.

Half-way down the canyon of South Mountain, near where it opens out upon the broad smiling valley west-ward, and just where the hills close nearest each other,

and the mass of forest is most dense; there, with mysterious resonance, leaps, as if struck by the wand of Circe,
the tumultuous water, over a bold jutting rock, into a
cavernous space below. Resting for a moment, and madly
twirling in its concave bed, again it pursues an onward,
harmless course. At one side the hill opens, forming a
thickly wooded ravine, where irregular masses of rock
rise to view. The whole scene is one of romantic interest.
Upon such a spot of nature's framing would some feudal
lord, in mediæval times have built his stronghold of a
castle with adamantine walls, where, enjailed behind
drawbridge and portcullis, he could bid defiance to all
foes, or retreat with ill-gotten spoils.

But, in the annals of the pioneer life, this place was for
a long time utilized by a saw-mill, with a house for the
miller attached to it, that was built over the waterfall.
Happily, there remains no vestige of all this at present.

It is said that, after the mill had become quite ruinous,
indeed uninhabitable, a very wicked old couple came and
lived there. The old woman, especially, was very malign.
She was often seen throwing stones at the passers-by on
the mountain road above her, and mingled with their last
glimpse of her elvish figure as she crouched in the shaky
door-way, would be heard her furious curses. She died as
she had lived, snarling and grumbling; and all the people
declared that certainly her spook would stay and haunt
this gloomy spot. Indeed, there was a general belief, that
any one so malevolent must be a witch, and quite given
over to the devil.

Well, her time of doom came, as has come through
all the generations, the appointed hour for all mortals.
The malicious old couple who had made mankind their
foe were no more. They had crumbled into dust, but the
ruinous mill still stood, an object of apprehension after
nightfall.

The countryman says that he was coming home after
dark, nursing his oozing courage by a brave whistling,
yet feeling none the better for having to pass the haunted
saw-mill, for haunted of course it was; yet saying to

himself that a man must be plucky all his hair stood on end by what he saw.

It had been very dark; but, just as he came opposite the evil spot, the moon broke through some dense clouds, and exposed to view a horrid spook. It was hard to describe it. It seemed such a huge and shapeless mass. It was big — very big; it had two horns that branched out wide like immense antlers, and, being horned, he knew by that same sign, it was a demon. It was shining white, and this made him think it must be the ghost of that wicked, little, ugly, old witch. How he hated her, as he thought of her giving all this worry, now she was no more! But there, in one indescribable heap, it lay, in that very door-way where the traveler had so often shuddered to hear her horrid imprecations.

This man is as strong as an ox; but he told us that he felt very weak for a minute, and his knees knocked together in a strange way; and then, with the brave thought that, if God was with him, nothing could harm him, he swiftly sped down the hillside. With one bound he cleared the little stream, and at the next moment he stood in the door-way — to find it was *a cow! An old white cow!!*

After we had all indulged in a good laugh at this encounter, in which the hero of the story joined most heartily, he resumed after a pause:

"Yet Mr. B—d and Mr. F—y were not so lucky, for what happened to them was really most strange." And then he narrated that these two farmers were coming up the Gorge one evening, slowly riding side by side, talking about their farms, the weather, and the prospect of the growing crops, when they were suddenly joined by a pedestrian, at a place on the road just opposite this old saw-mill. The men had been so earnestly engaged in conversation, that the manner of his appearance did not at first strike them as strange or unusual. But, presently, they began to feel very uncomfortable.

Their odd companion would at one moment walk close at the side of one horseman; then, without apparent means of transit, he would be between the two horses, although they rode side by side; again, at the next instant, he would be on the very opposite side, as if, indeed, he had walked through and through both horses at his pleasure and without an effort. This uncomfortable state of things went on for some little time, until the shadow had accompanied the farmers possibly half a mile.

They both became silent, and quite conscious that they were shadowed by no mortal man. One of the men finally got courage to speak to the phantom, and ask it what was wanted. There was no answer; a blank silence ensued, when the other man cried out, "Let us say our prayers, and ask the help of God."

At the instant the time that he uttered this incommunicable name, — a name adored by Heaven, and at which Hell trembles, — he was suddenly sent up in the air, with some violence, several feet from off his horse; yet he came down in the saddle again without being at all hurt. The demon had vanished. "It was always 'suspicioned,'" added our informant, "that there was once a murder at this place." And this last remark set us to thinking.

How passing strange it is that wherever there lingers but the suspicion of a trace of blood on the fair face of this old world of ours, how it will rust and tarnish the most beautiful scene, defacing Arcadian loveliness. The world is full of places where the marks of some blood struggle are pointed out as leaving an ineffaceable empurpled record. Thus the blood of Rizzio is said ever to appear. If the practice is deceptive, as some assert, in such cases, and these blood-stains are renewed, in order to impose on the credulity of the sight-seer, it only proves with greater force how deep-seated in the human heart is such belief.

When any particular house has become the scene of crime, especially if the circumstances surrounding the tragedy are such as to impress with horror the imagination, this house is at once branded by popular superstition. We must confess that we would not willingly occupy a room in any house whose walls had witnessed a murder. The taint would oppress the moral sense, and, to our apprehension, be more depressing than the danger of pestilence and disease.

As it is said of the witty Frenchman that his invariable question, whenever he heard of any suicide or other calamitous event was, "Who is she?" so sure was he that a woman must be the cause; so whenever one finds a spot darkened by superstitious fears, or where people, as they pass, "with shuddering horror pale," one may then know without the telling that this spot is a page defaced by crime on the eternal record.

There is such a house near South Mountain, said to have its *Poltergeist*, or disturbing devil. As to its exterior, this house is but a rude log structure, but within its rough walls a wicked man lived, and died the death of the wicked. He was a cooper by trade, and was surly and violent in disposition. He had a bitter quarrel with his only sister, and for years had not spoken to her. When this poor woman heard that he lay in the agonies of death, she could not refrain from coming to his bedside to beg him to be reconciled.

At this he fell into a furious rage, and glowered upon her in a savage way, pointing with feeble motion to a glass tumbler near. As she handed it to him, with a sudden force inspired by the demoniac passion that filled his soul, he made an expiring effort, as she bent over him, and hurled it at her face. But in that last deadly design he had expended the flickering light of life all in vain for his fiendish purpose of revenge, for his deadening grasp fell aimless, and sinking back, with frightful imprecations, and fixed and glaring stare, he expired in the very act of murderous intent. Since this tragic death-bed various families have lived in this house, only after a short time to leave it, declaring that they could not remain on account of the disturbances at night. Such is the gossip.

A lady, living within view, told us that, on one occasion, being up at midnight, and this house at the time without a tenant, she had seen it all aglow. Others affirm that pale, blue lights glance and flicker from window to window, and that the sound of *coopering* is heard, with the rolling about of barrels and the rattling of chains. For here, where sin and death shook hands, still rages "torment and loud lament." Truly, this world is replete in mysteries.

Even to the most commonplace people events so surprising often occur, that it has passed into a proverb that "truth is stranger than fiction." For what passer-by could ever in imagination connect this unpoetical old house with the weird or the fantastical?

And yet, if we consider life as designed by the hand of God, it is truly a glorious drama. There is a completeness in the design; and we who move upon the stage of this grand theatre often only play out our allotted part, without the slightest comprehension of the adjustment of means employed by the guiding course of Providence to form the unity. The actualities which make up our life, day by day, are yet not exactly what they seem; because the chain of our destiny is so delicately woven that no one link is disconnected with the past nor can be severed from the future. And so we fill up our probation, act upon act leading us insensibly, but surely, onward into eternity. Death guards the portals, which at last we reach, of the spirit land, and none may return more wisely to relive a second life on earth. But who shall divine *for thought* a resting-place?

And when to the eager, questioning soul arise visions of wonder, of beauty, and of harmony, the spirit knows no solemn boundary of death to arrest the impressions which come in palpable shapes to cheat the senses with their illusions. As we think over the narrow limit-time that, after all, separates the seen and the known from the unseen and the unknown, we are reminded of the strangest of the many strange recitals we have listened to.

And this, too, was of a haunted house, yet so wonderful and surprising, that it seems a revival of the old belief in the dreaded Sabbat. Alas, how many poor wretches have throughout all time been tortured into confessions of having attended these terrible festivities, where it was universally believed that witches, wizards, magicians, and demons met to perform with horrid incantations the most sacrilegious rites!

And here we have a recital of the meeting of the *Sabbat* in Maryland, and not fifty miles from Washington, — so true is it that the history of superstition, like the history of nations, is constantly "repeating itself."

It seems that a well-to-do farmer, having lived for a score of years in the comfortable two-story log house, built on the farm where he had planted and garnered in the successive crops that had enriched him, finally erected for himself and family a fine new brick house.

It is said that the ground upon which this new house was located was haunted; but of course, the unlucky man was ignorant of the fact that he had selected for his habitation the trysting place of demons. For how could the poor man for a moment have imagined that aught so fair to the sight as was this spot could be made foul with midnight orgies.

The situation was selected with a taste rarely exercised. The old house had been built in a valley, for shelter from the fierce blasts of winter; but the new brick house was solidly constructed, with a view to resist the cold winds, and placed on a pleasant eminence at the verge of a grove, where the majestic oak and towering poplar vied with the lustrous-leaved chestnut or the silver, quivering maple. In the autumnal days an iridescent glory of color charmed the eye. But on the precise place where the house was built were some gloomy pines and distorted and lightning-struck gum-trees, and these were cleared off the charred earth below, which they seemed only to incumber. Finally, the house being finished and made in complete readiness, it was occupied by the well pleased and happy family. Yet from that very first night in the much longed-for new home only blanched faces saw the morning light. And so it went on. Each night only brought a renewal of horrors, wild laughter, cries, shrieks, groans, and unearthly disturbances of every kind made the house an abomination. After some weeks of great suffering, the family were only too thankful to move back into the old, quiet restful home.

And then, the big, blank house stood desolate. Only a portion of the furniture, however, had been taken back to the log house, for it was quite too small to contain the appointments of the larger and finer new house. Some months intervened.

Strange and lurid lights would be seen in the house on the hill, if perchance the too curious eyes glanced that way at night, or now and then, the peaceful midnight was disturbed by discordant cries, and moans brought on the plaintive air.

The family had lost all hope of ever being able to reoccupy their new house.

One dark and stormy night a belated traveler knocked at the farmer's door. He asked for a night's lodging, for it seemed that neither he nor his horse could well go farther, — so weary were they. The farmer told the man that he was very sorry to appear so inhospitable, but that his house was small and too crowded with a large family to have a bed to spare. The horseman then said, I noticed some lights in a house on the top of the hill: I will in such case proceed.

"Do not so," said the farmer, "rather go to my comfortable barn, and sleep there beside your horse, for the house you have seen is haunted."

"Thanks," answered the stranger, "I will go on, God will protect me, and I fear not the power of evil spirits, for if they molest me, I will call upon His holy name."

So, this man of God bade the farmer good-by, and wended his way to the Haunted House, braver in his armor of simple faith, than was Odin when he described to the Niffhelian. Right into the mouth of hell marched he onward.

As he reached the house, the great hall-door flew wide open.

Nothing daunted, the good man entered, and ascending the stair-way, went into a pleasant room on the second floor. Here he found a bed, that seemed to invite repose, and being very tired, after having commended himself devoutly to God, he barred the door and lay down.

But not to rest or sleep, for no sooner, indeed, had his head touched the pillow, than the whole house seemed to be filled with an indescribable confusion of sound. He found himself in a very tower of Babel.

There appeared to be a large company arriving too, and a hurry of preparation, as if for some great festivity in progress. Presently he heard a step ascending the stairway. It advanced with deliberate purpose until his barred door was reached, which, without any apparent agency, at once flew open. The holy man arose.

He knew that the time had come to call upon God, for now he understood that, under whatever specious garb the image might appear, he really stood face to face with the Devil.

And yet his Satanic Majesty, if such he was, had every appearance of being a very polished gentleman of the nineteenth century.

Had he once lived in the dark ages, and worn horns and the cloven foot, these ugly adjuncts had been long cast aside as unfitted to the æsthetic tastes of the age. He was all too sagacious not to know that with the æsthete of the present day the machinery that once frightened the simple child of faith would only disgust, and not terrify the abstract lover of the beautiful, the philosophers who deny everything except their own impotent nihilisms, the political economists who raise their superstructures upon fallacies.

Therefore, as we have said, this personage was not an old-fashioned devil, whom one could mock and laugh at, but rather the Mephistopheles of the drawing-room. He was attired with precision in the conventional black dress-suit, white necktie, and boutonniére. He was, in fact, one who would figure as a *convive* of distinction at the approaching festivity.

He now accosted his guest with punctilious grace, and invited him to come below and join a party of friends who had arrived and were about to be seated at table. "In fact," he said, with a cold smile, "a champagne supper."

"Certainly," replied the traveller; "I am hungry as well as weary. I will go with you. Please lead the way." The two then descended the stairs, and entered the dining-room.

Could the sturdy farmer, who was safely sheltered in his log house in the valley below, but whose conscience, on account of his selfish act, banished sleep on that stormy night, for fear of what might happen to the traveller whom he had allowed to enter this den of demons, — could this plain farmer have seen the simple, unadorned room he had built with a view to solid comfort, thus transformed, he would have thought himself a lunatic. There hung suspended crystal chandeliers of symbolical design, around whose stems huge serpents twined, sending forth prismatic hues from many a scaly fold, their ruby eyes all lurid and their tongues of flame filling the room with swift, darting, forked, electric prisms and bluish tints, while the heavy odors of thousands of tropical plants in full bloom diffused an intoxicating and voluptuous languor. A table was extended the length of the apartment, and upon the snowy whiteness of the gossamer lace cloth were spread the luxuries of every clime.

Crystal as intangible as the spider's web, but cast in moulds of shapes that appealed to the passions, and transparent china, whose ravishing colors were blended with most consummate skill, but portraying scenes the good and pure would turn away from; every delicacy of the gastronomic art, recalling the banquets of Lucullus, — were placed upon this magic table; and wines of most delicious bouquet, as well as strong, hot, and spiced drinks of every clime from all the centuries past.

Yet these rare confections were set in diabolic forms, molded in contours that gave sacrilegious allusions to the sublime mysteries of faith. In the wine there was a symbol of blood; in the transcendent whiteness of the thin, rounded patens of bread, a sneer at most holy uses; and in the lamb-like shapes of the meats, the sinister taunt at innocence; the huge, jeweled cups were in mockery of the sacred chalice. Yet nowhere did even their demoniac hate dare do more than *sneer and suggest.* The awful semblance of some *babe of sacrifice* was held aloft in the centre, supported by cruel Gorgon heads and groaning Caryatides. Could it be human? Was it here, as always where hell revels, that blood was required.

All the Pagan rites demanded it; the *fetich* required it; and the Christian alone accepts the true meaning of vicarious sacrifice and the blood of the Atonement. And thus the Evil one mocks at the Incarnate one, until the *Dies Iræ!*

Meantime all the guests were assembled and in waiting for the Master and the Neophyte. What a close resemblance does it all bear to the world's assemblies! What a surprising phantasmagoria!

The women were robed in magnificent costumes of latest inventions, with neck and arms and figures enticing and statuesque, and bedecked with flashing jewels of the baleful opal, in whose shadow rested the black pearl. With painted faces, fluttering and dishevelled tresses, eyes of dreamy languor, lips of scarlet; while beneath the panting bosoms lay the cold, heavy hearts of stone.

And the men, ah, look throughout the length and breadth of the desolated homes of the land for these men, men built like some malefic idol, to harm and destroy, where self and the love of self have so corroded the very substance of their inner ego, that their natures would repel the true joys of Paradise, were the floodgates of Heaven opened and benediction showered upon them.

Upon their stony hearts, so hard, so cruel, cold, so polished, so pinched with money-getting, so grasping, all things good are lost, dead, ossified against all faith in aught divine. And of such have we in the mad whirl of our own world, lost like these men and women who composed that wanton assembly. Here was the prototype of the world's high festivals.

The Arch-demon whom all awaited entered with an air of easy grace, presenting their guest. The seat of honor and an unoccupied place beside it were theirs. With an exceeding refinement of courtesy the host offered his own place, as the one of first distinction, to the stranger, remarking that he would support him at the right.

"I accept your proffered hospitality on one condition," said the holy man, "and one alone," as he stood at the head of the table.

"And that condition must be strange indeed, if it o'ertaxes our courtesy," answered the host with frigid politeness.

"It is this," replied the man of God: "I never break bread without first giving thanks." A low, sibilant sound, as of hissing snakes, was the angry response! The flaming lights fade dead blue, the flowers exhale the sickening odor of decay, the bubbling wines shoot out angry fires, the meats suggest the sodden grave; the women grow at the instant, lean, old, and withered, with skinny arms and medusa locks, bending over their broomstick staff (before unseen); while the men, with distorted glare, grow beastly and fiendish.

The good, brave man, appalled at the awful changes, makes quickly in the air the grand symbol of redemption, the sign of the cross, while, with an air of sacred authority, as one of God's anointed, he calmly says, "In the name of the Triune God, I command you all to depart!"

One deafening crash, a dull explosion, a mingling of groans, sighs, yells, and curses, was followed instantaneously by blinding darkness. The room, the moment before presenting a scene of fairy delights, was filled with sickening sulphurous gases, and the earth shook under the thrill of the burden of sin retreating in dismay back to the cavernous depths of hell.

The *Sabbat*, as we read of it in all its magnificent

illusions of sorcery, had been tumultuously broken up by
the courageous act of one Christian soul who had faith,
and who knew that through the Cross one may conquer,
— *In hoc signo vinces.*

The holy man thereupon returned, giving praise and
thanks to God, to the log house of the farmer, who fell
upon his knees for very joy to see him come back alive;
for every one in the valley home had been startled by the
dull thud of the explosion, intermingled with cries of
anguish.

And yet, in the gray light of the early morning, there
the house stood unharmed and, what is more, purified.

From that very day, and ever since, the farmer and his
family have lived in it undisturbed; only they never forget to give thanks to God.

The crooning voice of the old woman had ceased, her
story is at an end; she had left us. Then, reclining on a
couch in the sultry heat of a mid-summer's day, quite in
the mood for introspection, we seem of a surety to
explore new realms of thought, when out of Dreamland,
into which we unconsciously enter, came this vision,
which we give as it was revealed to us, for it made us, as
it were, a personal actor in the illusory scene.

Methought I was *Eidolon*; and thus it was. I sat beside
my gentle mother, sweet flower of loveliness that she
was, — the cold dews of earth no longer chill her warm
heart, for now she blooms in Heaven. The time was
morning, and the day rejoiced in a light most deliciously
tempered. My heart, responsive to this happiness, thrilled
with gratitude to behold in these blessed sunbeams so
glorious a type of the beatific light. My mother understood me well. She saw that my soul thanked God; and

when she spoke, her tones were sad, as if grieved to remind me of the scene of mourning we were that day to witness.

"My child," she said, "this peerless day is chosen for the funeral of a woman who was lovely and gifted, bountifully enriched by nature, and caressingly wooed by fortune. I knew her from sweet infancy, through winning girlhood, and up to the full measure of beauteous and dignified maturity. She formed the perfect joy of doting parents. An immense wealth was freely lavished upon her, with which her unselfish and charitable nature dispensed a widespread happiness. In personal, in intellectual, and in moral loveliness, she was unequalled. She disdained no true womanly impulse, and her heart was tender and loving. Not many days have passed since Angeline became a bride. The man she chose to love, richly endowed with sensibility and genius, fully appreciated this woman, this wife of his soul.

"Society again renewed its acclamations; nor could the faintest shadow be perceived to mar so jubilant a future. Alas, in that moment so bright a star had culminated, for this day is her burial. And yet, my daughter, even in death has this bright creature a peculiar destiny. Magnanimous in all her actions, she has remembered the interests of science, and in her dying moments requested the learned man whose skill was powerless to save her life, to cause her death to be a benefaction, if possible.

"This man claims to have made a most wonderful discovery. He asserts that he has fathomed the arcana of nature to such an extent as to have discovered the power of extracting occult virtues, through the means of certain chemical combinations heretofore unknown. These powerful agencies produce a liquor which he calls "Quintessence of Life," because, in order to compose this substance, he evolves out of nature a revivifying principle inherent of her laws which existed as the normal condition of things in Eden. Through this perennial impulsion the Creator had destined for his perfect world a never-failing and full vigor. But the blight of decay, through sin, fell upon this fair creation. Yet this heavenly essence in nature, formerly coexistent with the visible presence of God on earth, could not be annihilated, because it was an effusion of divinity. It still throbs through every pulse of nature; it still forms the heart, the animating cause of all manifestations of life through every grade of development short of that life which is the breath of God direct, and forms the human soul.

"When Eden bloomed, no pestilential influence counteracted its full expansion as now, and then an entire harmony through all creation was the result. Could this essence be spiritualized, it would assimilate to seraphic love. But sublime as are its ordained effects, creating sympathies and attractions which preserve the world from instant destruction, yet it is a pure symbolism. With what awe do we trace its existence from the massive foundations of the everlasting mountains, descending to the verdant valleys, pausing to view the gushing rivulets, the majestic rivers, and the mighty sway of the ever-agitated ocean. So also do we contemplate it in the so-called instinct of animals, which now perverted does not make manifest the original design of creation, but which, in its pure primeval sources, breathes forth so much angelic sweetness, that we are told the lion and the lamb could dwell in peace together.

"Science, like the morning sun, explores the firma-ment, penetrates with its rays the most secret places, and rushes on in its impetuous career up to the full zenith of knowledge. Science has at last seized this quintessence of life, which is a thousand thousand times more volatile than any known substance. When galvanism was discovered to be capable of producing a seeming reanimation, it was but the faintest shadow of the power contained within the surprising range. It is supposed that this elixir, applied after death, acts upon our bodies with such a potency as to seem to hold the parted soul once more in obedience to the sense's laws. This effect can be produced but once in each person; nor can it be of long duration that our bodies can be even apparently reanimated after death through the infusion of this essence, which brings all things into immediate sympathy with nature. The lovely bride, whose burial we are to-day invited to witness, has desired that this experiment, never yet tested; shall be made previous to her interment; and her wishes, sacred in the eyes of affection during life, are to be equally respected in death."

My mother's words, always received with filial tenderness, had now a strange power over me; and as she unfolded the idea of this sage, I felt as if awakening from a long dream, and ready to realize his weird vision to the full extent.

And so, like one arising from a bed of sloth, I wrapped my mantle round me and walked forth with my mother to join the procession of mourners. In nothing did the funeral arrangement differ from that usual for those who accompany the spirit pilgrim to earth's last resting-place who now reposed so statue-like in death, was borne upon a bier, whose only covering was violets, — meek-eyed violets, whose grateful perfume she had of all flowers best loved while living. The spot selected and prepared for obsequies so peculiar was a marvelous creation of art, and in its adaptation to the wonderful solemnities which awaited us, fully evinced the idolatry of affection that had spared no effort to find an adequate expression.

Cradled in the bosom of a verdant and gentile ravine we found a grotto, fitted rather for the pose of the joyous and light-hearted than for the stern and bleak companionship of death. The coffin of this beautiful woman was sculptured out of purest alabaster, in touching allusion to the custom of the ancients, who preserved their choicest perfumes in vases of this material. Angeline was placed with tender care upon this couch of dazzling whiteness, robed in her lustrous bridal satin, which has been made, at her own request, with *so entire a maiden modesty that in such drapery could be endured without shrinking the ordeal of death and final judgment.* Exquisite rose-colored shells completely encased this charming retreat, and they were disposed with so surprising a skill as to diffuse the most enchanting light, and at the same time produce the most bewitching sounds. The softest Æolian tones floated on the fragrant air, laden with the choicest odors of sweet-breathing flowers. Beside her marble tomb was placed the harp of Angeline, the death-won bride. During life her skill and power over, her love of, this sacred and poetic instrument had been a special gift, the pleasing means through which her lofty soul had oft expressed its inspirations. It was the expectation of the sage that, could he succeed in reanimating Angeline, she would again find in her loved harp a medium of utterance for the emotions of her departed soul. Now the awful moment of trial approaches, and the learned man applies the subtle essence to her icy lips. Angeline slowly arises from the tomb, with no painful effort, but with the quiet and simple grace so characteristic of her movements during life.

How exceedingly fair she was! Each feature was so delicately chiseled, and her hair fell in richest masses of golden ringlets, like a halo encircling her beauteous face. She leaned forward, and seemed to lovingly clasp her harp. As if responsive to the slightest touch, the noble harp gave forth its sounds. At once her pliant fingers, full of a sympathetic ardor, swept the chords, while her prayerful gaze was directed heavenward, as if assisting the angelic hosts to praise the Lord. I felt she pictured in perfect harmony Elysian joys. Wave upon wave of melody rolled over me with overpowering force. And now I knew how no human ear could bear so full a delight. Excessive rapture releases the imprisoned spirit, and I understood that my soul was leaving its tenement of clay, thus guided onward to its highest good. I comprehended, too, that among all the surrounding throng, my being sympathized with hers in deepest measure. Suddenly she ceases, regards me, advances, and, extending her arms, holds me closely embraced. I shudder, benumbed with intense cold, and seek to release myself from this sure grasp of Death.

"*Ah, Eidolon; not death, but life,*" she whispers to me. "Eternal life, seraphic love, endless joy, hope lost in fruition, — *life in death, my Eidolon!*"

Chapter VI

WITCHCRAFT

SOUTH MOUNTAIN shares the world's fever of vain longing for gold, and the mysterious finding of gold forms the subject of many of its sorcerous recitals.

In all ages, all countries, and all climates, these wild fancies have had a place. In the dreamy Orient are the fabled perennial fountains ever filled with liquid gold. The transmuting of baser metals into gold formed the hope of the visionary alchemist of the Middle Ages. The expectation these experimentalists had of thus gaining boundless wealth, with the vast power growing out of it, lured these men on through a wide range of investigation, out of which, after all, a beneficent Providence gave back a richer harvest than the production of gold. For out of the studies born of this restless desire, was the foundation laid for the noble art of chemistry.

But the impatient and sordid desires of the mass of people do not wait for the results of investigation or of experiment. In the exciting phantasms of sorcery their ardent wishes are fed with a more congenial, if not more certain pabulum.

The first superstition we have noticed regarding money, seems to be connected with what doubtless are some natural exhalations of luminous gases. We are confirmed in this opinion from an incident told us in quite a boasting way by the narrator, as a proof of his great courage.

There was in one of the upland cleared valleys of the mountain a forty-acre field, which had been at one time partially under cultivation.

Presently it was bruited about that in this field raged some fatal fire, which like the *Tomb Fires* of the Scandinavian, portended disaster to those who would approach too near,

The wonder grew with what it fed upon, and presently no one was willing to work in the field.

Especially on wet, dark nights this demon could be very distinctly seen. It appeared to have horns, and was fiery, but without a head.

There is a sect on South Mountain that annually hold what are called "bush meetings," because they take place, we suppose, in the open air, and doubtless, originally, where the thickets gave a certain shelter from the weather, if need be.

This man told us that one night, as he was returning from one of these meetings accompanied by the "women folks" of his family, he found it convenient, in order to shorten the route, to pass near this field. To this the women objected, which, of course, made him all the more determined (with that "set" way men so often have) to go in that direction, and by no other road.

They were in a little spring wagon, driven by a well-worked farm horse, whose exuberance of spirit had been checked by the practical uses of life, until he had become very sedate and sensible.

But sure enough, when they arrived at this noted place, to use the man's expression, "there the thing was." The horse snorted, and gave signs of being vicious, the women trembled, but our adventuresome man was bent on finding out the mystery. So, in spite of the entreaties of the women, he left them to "mind the horse," and he went to look after that scaly monster. Selecting a stout club from the woods that bordered the field, he resolutely marched up to the place, which seemed as he approached still nearer to be a mass of quivering fire. Nothing daunted, however, this sturdy mountaineer gave this horrible-looking object a right valiant knock with his strong stick, which caused the rotten wood of the old stump to fly in all directions. The fantastic shape had been produced by two knots and a forked prong sticking out of the center.

The next day the place was carefully examined, and the stump which had assumed such an alarming aspect was found to be full of what is called *fox-fire*. After this was removed there was no longer a luminous appearance there, and the field lost its terrors and was cultivated as before. But this is, we believe, perhaps the only instance narrated to us where credulity has been disturbed by the discovery of natural causes at work.

On the contrary, a sort of *cromlech,* or circle of fiery stones, worthy to find a place in the conjurations of Ossian, are believed in.

We are confidently informed that when one sees a pile of fire on the meadow-grass after night, one must be sure to go and rake up the coals, for they will, when thus gathered, turn to silver.

O—e one night saw such a fiery circle, and he went to it and got a hat-full of silver, But at this juncture, when he was making haste to be rich, a swarm of snakes issued forth and compelled him to beat a hasty retreat, nor could he ever again find the lucky place. And so the "adder's fork and blindworm's sting," are left to guard this hidden treasure.

Another similar piece of good fortune was narrated to us. A woman was walking in a field at night, when she noticed what seemed to be coals of fire. She at once went to the place and picked up the coals, out of curiosity, supposing it to be what the country people call "natural fire." These she took home with her, and when they had quite cooled off, they proved to be silver.

An odd story was told us of a very lazy man on the mountain. So indolent, indeed, was he that he might just as well have crept into a cave or any subterranean cavern and slept twenty or fifty years as did Rip Van Winkle; nor would the world have been the loser. This slothful man had a scolding wife who, by her never-ceasing activity, happily restored the domestic balance. This "gude-wife" was, as a matter of course, ever berating her good-for-nothing spouse on account of his consummate laziness. Finally, one day at high noon, finding this laziest of men still asleep, she made a great clamor. "You are like a night owl," she said; "only fit to be hooted at."

At this gentle speech, slowly turning over in the bed, with a great yawn, he said, "Never you mind, woman, my laziness will make me rich yet." And thereupon the sluggard, as if exhausted with the effort, settled himself very snugly in bed for "a little more folding of the hands for sleep." His wife, exasperated beyond all bounds, rushed out of the house. She went to an old stump, and from the decayed center dug out a basketful of what seemed to be black pinching bugs. Then returning, she threw them in a heap upon this dronish man. *Then, these beetles all changed into silver.* Whereupon, once more with dilatory sloth turning over in his bed, he mumbled with a huge yawn, "Did I not tell you my laziness would make me rich yet?" Although we have not as yet had the sagacity to discover any special moral to this story, yet we must confess to somewhat of pardonable pride in the recital; for we doubt very much that if Washington Irving, of revered memory, were to come back and charm the world anew with the quaint humor of his inimitable narratives, that he could find just such another exquisite conception of a lazy man. For let it be noticed with due admiration, that even the magic *gold* showered upon him did not excite him, or have other effect in arousing his unconquerable sloth than to call forth a more prolonged yawn and the satisfaction of settling himself snugly for another sleep!

It is said if one hides money it will bring bad luck. In proof of this, we were told about a "hired girl" who, while sweeping, picked up a "fip-penney-bit;" that is, a small silver coin of the value of six and one quarter cents. This money she hid upon a shelf over the door. Soon after which she died. Then she came back in the form of a white sheep, and stood in the doorway. The people of the house *recognized her* wraith, and asked her what she wanted. Then she straightway made answer that she came back "to tell of the money hidden on the shelf over the door." We are told that after that "open confession" the poor wraith was "laid," and never looked sheepish any more.

"Yes, yes," added the old crone, shaking her head; "money'll bring anybody back!!"

Then, to confirm her statement, she narrated a very remarkable case in illustration of this profound truth.

Once upon a time, the precise date of which was not given, there lived a very rich woman, somewhere up on a high farm on the table-land of South Mountain. She hoarded her riches, and then hoarded the usufruct; nor would she spend even so much as to make herself comfortable. She was also too miserly to help the poor people who had such a hard struggle for existence, and who lived in the huts of the mountain forest around her. Absolutely she would not spend money.

Everything prospered with her; her flocks of sheep increased; her dairy of fine cows was splendid; all the "live-stock" around her multiplied; the crops were abundant; the orchards laden with fruit, and plenty reigned. And yet she lived as might a pauper, this miserly old woman. As the Lord had given, so the time came when the Lord took away, for presently death reaped the final harvest.

The young heir, now jubilant master of the farm and a reckless spendthrift, had taken hilarious possession. Now, there lived on the place, hired as a farm hand, a very poor man, who was driving a farm wagon for the master of the farm. One day, as he was plodding his toilsome way through a dense piece of woods at no great distance from the former home of this miserly woman, he came to a little mountain stream that ran across the rude road, over which was a roughly constructed bridge of planks hewn out of rude logs.

Just as he reached this bridge, the hitherto quiet horses became very restive, snorted, reared, and could not be forced forward. He then perceived, standing near the bridge, the wraith of the former mistress of the place. She motioned to him with looks distressed to stop. He stood stock-still. Had he been in Wales, doubtless he would have fled from the *Tan-We*, as harbinger of evil. But our woodsman had good courage.

The pale ghost then, stooping down, raised one end of the plank of the bridge, which the man then for the first time perceived to be loose. From under this loose board she took a key. Then she glided onward into a cedar thicket near the wayside. Here she removed a little flat stone. When, under this stone was seen a little door, nicely fitted into a cleft of the rock at the mouth of a small cave. With the key she opened this door. The man saw that the cave was full of silver. This was the wicked hoarding of a lifetime, — the "talents" lent her by her Lord and Master, which this unfaithful servant had "hid under a bushel." Then the sorrowing wraith uplifted a piteous face, and in imploring tones said to the man, "In mercy to my soul, take all this: leave not so much as one coin, that I may go to my rest."

Then the poor farm hand took back his team to the farmer who employed him, and said to him: "Here is your team. I do not have to work any more for another, for I am richer than you are."

At this all the other farm hands jeered at him, saying, "This man has indeed lost his senses. He has gone crazy!" Whereupon he soon left South Mountain; but sure enough, presently he was heard from in the far West, where he had bought a splendid farm and was reputed to be very rich.

We have only to add our sincere hope that the reader of this thrilling adventure may receive the story with the same spirit of undoubting credence with which it was told to the writer.

The Rhabdomantic art, or the method of divining with the rod, a mystic rod, supposed to call forth nature from her lethargy, as did the Caduceus of Mercury, to which the rocks responded, — this art is not known to the mountain adepts. This divining-rod is a forked branch of some particular wood, and is carried in a certain even, level way in the hand of the *seer*. The ground is then carefully explored, and when the spot sought for is reached the rod inclines of itself downwards. We had ourselves a somewhat curious experience as regards the use of this rod. We desired to have a well dug adjacent to our barn, and designated a place which looked moist and loamy, and likely to yield a favorable result. The well-diggers, however, disapproved our choice, but continued to dig until they had reached a depth of thirty feet. The prospect here was so discouraging that we left it to the men at work to proceed according to their usual forms. They then got a divining-rod, and, after moving about with it for some time, located a spot as favorable for water, from the dipping of the rod in that direction. In effect, at a depth of some fifty feet a remarkably fine stream of water was reached. Of course, every such instance is considered as proof absolute of the importance of consulting the divining-rod in order to find water.

Doubtless there is a secret of nature back of this manifestation. Perhaps this may be found in the magnetic properties of some trees, which might readily cause their branches to incline so as to indicate water; or the magnetism which some metals exert. These facts may only be connected with the same power that makes the magnet of such value to man. But we turn away from the tempting field of speculation, our province, as we have before stated, being that of a narrator. The philosophy of Magic we leave in abler hands and to the *savants*.

We now approach with great diffidence the legends of witches and of their operations.

When we reflect on the damnable catalogue, in the world's history, of the cruelties inflicted upon poor humanity, the tortures, the ordeals by fire, by water, by hot iron, to which the accused were subjected; of the friendless, who have been crushed, and the malicious, who have gratified deadly hatred under thy name, O Witchcraft, we tremble as we touch the stained hem of thy cabalistic robe. O malignant Demon! Under what protean shapes do we find this evil one which forestalls all reason. What a gloomy procession, as we behold the ancient Magi, the necromancers, astrologers, witches, warlocks, familiar spirits, sooth-sayers, conjurers, — onward they troop, with forked, lying tongues, with enchantments, and with scribes to indite black-letter falsehoods.

Then, like some deadly upas-tree, spreading forth its vast and pleasing ramifications, inviting to a repose under its shadow, we see other victims fascinated, but not overcome by the poisonous influence. Notable scholars, who have held firm faith in the secret sciences; great warriors of all ages, consulting the sibylline leaves of fate; and even the good and the wise, yielding at times like children to the wondrous charm. Then the long list of captivating romances, such as turned the brain of Don Quixote; after that, the staid belief of Wesley; and later on, the bloody page the Puritans left on New England history, in their zeal against witches. Verily, we grow dazed, and try to grope our way out of this obscure wilderness. But we are no longer amazed, nor do we think it irrelevant or wonderful, to find on the brow of old South Mountain the mystic veil, wrought of the web of lingering tracery of all these potent illusions.

We know, too, that Nature molds men to receive impressions from her surrounding scenes which influence their perceptions. In the mountains, most of all, men become imbued with the sense of the mysterious. Of course, among the very ignorant this sense crops out in the lowest forms, and, divested of romance, has only the semblance of the puerile.

The nomenclature is familiar here to all; and we often hear alluded to, as if of undoubted reality, witches, wizards, witch-conjurers, and doctresses; such and such persons being pointed out to you as wielding these extraordinary powers.

The first story of this kind told us was of a very disagreeable landlord. This man was a wizard, and had rented a house he owned down in the beautiful Middletown Valley, that stretches far away from the base of South Mountain; and he wished for some reason to get rid of his tenant. Very likely because his tenant did not pay his rent. But finding the occupants obstinate, and "possession being nine-tenths of the law," and not wishing the perplexity, expense, or uncertainty of a lawsuit, he cast a spell" over the house, which made it too uncomfortable for the tenant to be willing to remain. This astute landlord was consequently soon left in possession, without being obliged to resort to harsher methods of eviction.

We beg permission in this connection to suggest to the British Premier that, inasmuch as the indomitable Irish tenants have good faith in warlocks and their dreaded agency, that the employment of a constabulary force of *wizards*, duly accredited as such, with big yellow diplomas, upon which shall be painted the English lion rampant, and with permission to exercise all the old methods in vogue in the Elizabethan Era, would result in more speedy evictions than the present brutal methods in force. It is only necessary to make the Celtic paupers who will not, because they cannot, pay the rents of their mud shanties, understand that a *Banshee* harries the hovel, or a witch puts poison-papers at the roots of the "praties," and it will be found that these same untamable paupers will prefer starvation, freezing, and famine fever to living in league with the Evil One.

However, as we have not as yet given the needed careful attention to this very complicated question of political economy, we do not venture to advise, but merely *suggest* the adoption of these incorporeal measures! Be this as it may, the sequel of this story is very fine, and, like some other story-tellers we wot of, we were flying off at a tangent and quite omitting the point of the joke, which was this: —

The moment the persecuted tenant had vacated, it is affirmed that a little old gray-haired, wizened man, with *trembling fiery fingers,* was seen to go three times round and round and round the house throwing wizard's ashes, — doubtless of a singed cat, — and all in the three highest names. Thus the "spell" was taken off, and the house purified and made ready for the next tenant, who would be undisturbed so long as he paid his rent.

We have a particular affection for this warlock with the fiery fingers, inasmuch as he knew how not only to cheat the lawyers, but likewise the Devil. For it will be noticed that he reclaimed under the invocation of the Most Holy Trinity that which he had called upon the Demon to lay waste.

Yet probably, as we only see such little shreds of things in this world, that when we come to know something more about this matter in the next, we shall then see that, after all, the devil got his due in good season, and will finally fly off with the soul of the wizard in his clutches.

There is a pleasant belief on South Mountain that any one who desires in a business way to make a regular contract, can go and sell himself to the Evil One. To be sure, we have often noticed in Washington and elsewhere, that there was every appearance, if not legal evidence, of a similar contract being made. Yet we were not aware that they were accredited in red-tape form to their real source. But mountain air being very blue and transparent, we are more apt to have the essence of facts, stripped of courtly disguises. An instance was narrated to us which explains quite clearly the *modus operandi* in such cases.

Sallie S——s, a rattling young girl, who lived on the hills between South-Mountain-House and Myersville, took a fancy in her foolish young noddle that it would be "great fun" to be a witch. Thereupon she went to Granny H——, and said to her, "Granny, I've come to have you make me a witch."

"Now, Sallie, do you really want to be a witch, for sure and certain?"

"Yes, Granny; for sure and certain."

"Well, then, you must wait till Friday. Then, when you get up, don't wash your face, but come to me by high noon, and I promise you, you shall see the old gentleman."

Let the reader mark *the respectful* epithet, "the old gentleman!"

These injunctions were carefully complied with, and the unwashed, unkempt damsel presented herself at midday at the hut of Granny H—.

Soon after she got there a little old man came in and at once accosted the young girl.

"So you want to have a trade with me, eigh?"

Somewhat frightened at his brusque manner, she timidly answered, "Yes."

Then said he, "Sit down on the floor, put one hand on the top of your head and the other hand on the soles of your feet, and say — 'All that is between my two hands belongs to the Devil.'"

So the girl sat down on the floor, did as she was bid, and said, "All that is between my two hands belongs to God."

At this unexpected termination the old man gave a hideous howl, like the bark of a dog, and vanished. But he left the room so filled with sickening gases, that the poor child swooned away; and the old witch being very angry, picked her up and threw her, insensible as she was, out in the yard in front of the house. Here the open air revived her. But we are assured that she never went to see Granny H— any more, nor has she since then ever had any wish to become a witch.

It is said of this same wicked old woman, that she delighted in casting her "spells" over the cows of her neighbors.

Our informant told us that her uncle had nine cows,

but that this witch having cast a spell over them all, not a bucket of milk could be got. At the time of the milking all would seem to be right, but when the crocks would be set away in the spring-house, and they would be ready for the churning, blood would be found settled in the bottom of every crock.

There was another family. The old father was sick and bed-ridden, and the two daughters depended on the sale of the butter they made. Presently some "charm" was cast on the milk, and they could not bring butter in the churning. It was "suspicioned" that this same hateful old Hecate had done the mischief.

It was considered very dangerous to make this "witch-conjurer" angry, and although every one hated her, they feared her more. So generally, whatever she asked for she got.

It is related that one hot day, passing that way, she stopped at a farm-house and asked for a drink of milk. The day was very sultry, and the milk had turned sour. This made the witch very angry, so she cast a "spell" on the two cows. Soon after this she went away, when the cows began to run round in a ring, bawling out, and remaining in great misery until they died.

But on another occasion a still greater calamity is said to have resulted from the displeasure of this witch.

She had stopped at a farm-house and asked for a drink of cream. The women of the house bade her go away, saying they had no cream to give her. Now, there stood two pots of cream in the spring-house, ready for the churning. This house was a nice cool place, the windows, being well guarded against flies with wire gauze, and it was kept locked. The next morning the place was found full of flies, and a dead pig in the cream, although there were no pigs known to be on the farm at that time. Two cows were also dead, and one horse, all of which, as may be imagined, was a great loss to these poor people.

"But," added my informant, with an air of great satisfaction, "my aunt killed the witch-conjurer."

"Killed her!" we exclaimed with horror, fearing to be

made the unwilling confidant of some secret murder. "What *do* you mean?"

"Well, it came about in this way: My grandfather (an illustrious ancestry!) was a witch-conjurer, and he taught his son's wife. Now, my aunt said, 'Granny H. is doing too much harm, and she must be stopped, and she would put an end to her the next time there was any more mischief done.' Not long after that, when Aunt Kitty went out to milk, the milk came from the cows all '*cruddled*' and mixed with blood. So she milked them all dry, and as fast as she milked she poured the milk into a trough for hogs. Then she threw into the milk red-hot stones, and filled up the trough with thorns and briers cut fine. All the time she was doing this she *said the words*, and called on the three highest names. Well, the next day the witch was found dead in her bed. She was all bruised with stones and cut with briers and thorns."

"But," said we, "what did your aunt have to do with that?"

"Why, don't you see," said the crone, "when you can get the milk they have bewitched, you can kill them through their own spells, in that way."

"Yes, we understand that as you explain it; but what were *the words* your aunt used?"

"Ah," said the crone, gravely shaking her head, "that is what I cannot tell you; because no woman may tell a woman, or no man tell a man. But a woman can tell a man, or a man can tell a woman: that is a witch rule."

We were quite prepared for that answer, having so often been assured of the same thing before. This is really a curious superstition, and one rigidly enforced among these people. We can in no-wise trace any cause for such a custom, nor could any one give us the least reason for the rule, except that blind one, which, like an ultimate appeal, closes all argument, namely, "because *it is so*."

Happily, however, in consequence of our various conversations with the old men as well as the old women of the Mountain, we have attained to the knowledge of many curious "spells."

We have also been told of other so-called witches who have "laid spells" on cows, through supposed malice at some fancied offence.

In one case we were told that the milk would not run through the strainer, and when the finger was run round in the strainer, the milk was *"cruddled"* and bloody, with such consistence that one could cut it with a knife, and there was a skin formed over it, — all of which, we are informed, are certain signs of its being bewitched. In this instance, fortunately, the people whose cow had been tampered with, knew how to undo the "spell." They therefore poured the evening's milking in a hog-trough, and put in wedges of hot iron, all the while "saying the words." Of course, in the form of these "words" is the secret.

We are told that this same witch, being asked to give proof that she was really a witch, took an empty basket and filled it with chips of wood, and this openly and without attempt at concealment. She then placed the basket in the middle of the room, on the floor; where-upon she described a circle round it, in the inner round of which she walked three times, all the while "saying the words." This being done, she sat down upon the chips in the basket. After some three minutes mumbling of "words" she arose, and a number of *blue mice*, of a kind never seen before, ran out of the basket and about the room.

Once a Mr. H— went to see this witch, and offered her five dollars to show him some witch trick. Whereupon she went to a bureau in the room, took out of the drawer a clean, folded towel, unfolded it, and shook it out at full length, that he might see that there was nothing in it. She then hung this towel on a nail in full view, and, saying "the words," milked out of the dry folds of the towel, without apparent effort, a quart of milk.

All this witchery we have related has only affected inanimate things or animals; but again, other "spells" are cast showing a deeper malice against people.

Mrs. L——e told us that one night, being awake at the time, she had a sudden and sharp blow given her, that drew blood on her arm. Her scream awoke her husband, who at once arose, lighted a candle, and they made instant and careful search. Nothing could be found; but the hurt place on her arm looked like a cut. They thought it was a malicious attempt of a witch, and that witch a neighbor! Certainly not a very complimentary opinion of one's visiting acquaintance!

We were told of a child that suddenly became bewitched, and screamed incessantly until, a wizard being sent for, the "spell" was taken off by him, and the child quieted.

One instance closely resembles the *spirit-rapping* nuisance, although it was affirmed to be a case of witchcraft. The two are at least first cousins, we opine.

A negro girl, ten years of age, whose name was Smith, was "bound out" by her mother for seven years' service to one of the Mountain cottagers. The child resisted the arrangement, and declared that she would not leave home. But she was forced to go, and was given the charge of a baby in her new home. Presently it happened that whenever the baby was handed to her, her hands would drop, and the baby roll off on the floor, and keep rolling over and over. If the infant was laid upon the bed, the bed-clothes would roll off the bed with the child wrapped in them; and if the girl was placed beside the cradle to rock the baby, cradle, baby, and all would roll over and over. There was great consternation. The neighbors all came in to see the wonder, and to consult as to what was best to be done; and it was finally agreed that the negress was bewitched, and that she must be sent home. They accordingly sent her back, when quiet was restored.

The man who told us this said it happened many years ago on South Mountain; but it has a close resemblance to many cases of what are called spirit disturbances, or of the spirit-rapping class.

One story told us is a striking proof of the power of

imagination. A boy of fifteen, the son of a widow, had given his mother much trouble, being very insubordinate. One day this poor woman said to her wilful son, "Never mind, William, if you are so wicked, some day the bad man will come after you." The boy went out jeering, and saying, "I ain't keeping any count of what you say." Soon after he came in, looking very pale, and said, "Mother, I must die; I've seen a ghost." He at once took to his bed, fell ill, never rallied, and died soon after. This happened some twelve years ago, and the names and the exact locality were given us.

Indeed, the people who told us these various stories have always very freely mentioned the names of people, and quite often they are those of persons whom we have met. But of course we do not intend to make our narratives so personal.

This remark reminds us of an absurd incident which occurred at South-Mountain-House. Our very phlegmatic Dutch farmer said to us one morning, in a solemn way, that he had been awakened the night before by an attempt to enter the house; that he could distinctly see a man trying to force the window below his room. "Why did you not shoot the burglar?" we asked, "since you saw him in the very act of trying to break into the house." "I could not do that," was the deliberate answer, "for I was sure that I *recognized an acquaintance!*" So the dear public will understand that, in refraining from giving names, we spare, "our acquaintance!"

There exists, also, another curious impression as to an evil practice of witches, and that is of their victims being what is called "pressed" or "ridden" to death.

A man told us that, if one suffered from being "pressed," the way to undo the spell was this: When you go to bed, cross your hands three times, then cross your feet three times at the moment you feel something "pressing" you. Then, if you can, keep your "weather eye" open, as the sailors say, and you will not fail to see a black cat running up your bed; when fizz goes the witch on a broomstick up the chimney! We would suggest that where these tricks of witchcraft are of common occurrence, it will perhaps be safer not to fill the open chimney with a sandbag, as they do in the country, so as not to intercept the egress of the witch. This counter charm, as told us, is a pleasant and easy thing to do; and with the addition of saying one's prayers three times, can be safely recommended by way of asserting one's independence of all witchcraft.

Another thing to bear in mind is, that every one should be very careful what they do on Friday, because that is the day upon which the Evil One has greatest power. We have noticed in all the stories that have been confidentially told us, that Friday is "witch day." No doubt exists about that.

Of course, the Christian mind will at once perceive the reason why Friday is a day of malediction, being accursed, because on that day the powers of evil wreaked their utmost malice against High Heaven; but cherished by the Christian heart as inexpressibly dear, for then its redemption was consummated. And yet, until this world shall be consumed in that awful Day of Wrath, wherever the power of the Evil One is feared, he is given Friday as that hour of triumph, when as "an ugly serpent he forestalls the way." So, "forewarned is forearmed."

Some thrilling adventures relating the power of witches to "ride" their victims or "press" them to death have been related to us, of which we select one.

Three young men were hired as farm hands by a well-to-do farmer. Now the farmer's wife was a witch, but no one knew it. When these young men went to live on this farm they were strong and in good health. Presently, one of the three, who had at first been most vivacious and hilarious, began to droop in a very unaccountable way. He looked worn and sick, and although he had an immense appetite, he evidently was not nourished, but grew thinner and thinner day by day. After a time, the companion who was his bedfellow said to him, "What's the matter, Jake? You grow as thin as a "coon." "I can't help it," replied Jake despondingly, "I'm ridden to death." And so he told his friend the weary truth that every night an old hag came, led him out, put a halter round his neck, and rode him like a horse "athwart the thickets lone." "She stayed not for brake and she stopped not for stone" until he would be brought back more dead than alive in the morning. "Very well," said the friend, "I'll fix it tonight. We will change places in the bed, and when she comes to me, I'll attend to her."

That night the witch came as was her habit, and seized, as she supposed, her victim, put the magic bridle in his mouth, got on his back, and rode him out. What a wild ride it was! She rode him like all the furies, "o'er moor, o'er marsh, mid reedy fens widespread." Finally she came to a deeper brook, when, dismounting, she was about to hitch the bridle to a tree. At this, seizing the opportunity he had waited for, he snatched the magic bridle from his own neck, and, despite her struggles, succeeded in fastening it in her mouth. Then, jumping on her back, he rode her quickly to the village smithy, where calling up the laborious smith, as in pressing need, he had four shoes nailed on; that is, he had her hands and feet shod. He then rode home, took off the magic bridle, let her go, and went back to his room.

The next morning they were told that the farmer's wife was very sick. Some days later she died, and after her death it was found that she had horse-shoes driven through her hands and feet.

There is something especially appalling amid the puerile simplicity of this story, in the resemblance of the tragic suffering of nails through the hands and feet to the torments inflicted upon our dear Saviour. The images of the passion of the Redeemer, of the redemption, the types of the atonement, are everywhere written upon the world's history in ineffaceable characters of living, burning light.

After having narrated so many dreadful stories of the pranks of the Demon, it is refreshing to close this chapter by giving a conversation *verbatim* that we had with a poor woman. She lived with a brood of small children in a fragment of a house which only retained a portion of its roof.

During the battle of South Mountain a shell had torn away the foundation of this house on one side, and the broken windows and swinging doors wore a crazy and dismantled look. During all the long years since this ruin came upon them they had lived exposed to every rain, and really shelterless in every storm. God alone knows how they had borne it all in the long, cold winters. Here we found them, although we are happy to say they now have a comfortable cabin.

What we wish is to give, in her own inimitable words, this poor woman's account of their trust in Providence. She said to us: "Whin the shell kim an busted in one side of the house, jist at the foundation, an' the children cried out, 'Muz, ain't you afeerd to stay? I sez, 'No, children, *thar's a Providence, an' ef He chooses*, our house can jist stay tilted up on three legs as well as ef we put it on four, an' I'm goin' to sleep.' *An' we all slep' that night*, an' we lived in this house, until you kim up here, jist as you see'd us; an' whin the storms kim that blowed down the big trees, they niver hurt a hair of our heds. An' whin the Jidge kim by, he sez, 'I niver see'd the like of this afore,' whin I up an' tells him, '*You bet, Jidge, thar's a Providence.*'"

Chapter VII

MAGIC CURES AND THE BLACK BOOK

"When we consider life, 'tis all a cheat,
For fooled with hope, men favor this deceit"

AS the Persians had their Magi, the Indians of the
Orient their Gymnosophists, and the Gauls their Druids,
so South Mountain claims a rude form of divination.

It has its poetic and superstitious magic. Zoroaster
taught that certain herbs, stones, and other inanimate
objects, could be endowed with supernatural qualities;
and we find ancient magicians making use of love-
philters and of mysterious unctions and slaves. Astrology,
too, claimed occult properties in numbers.

So has South Mountain had its Archimagus to make
use of magic means, and its wise men and women who
are said to have the power of healing. At times fire is the
Sechinah, and at other times the emanation or virtue lies
in other elements.

Superstition, in these cases, takes the place of the long
sought-for alkahest, and acts as a universal dissolvent. It
explains all things.

We now propose to give in detail various superstitious
practices in vogue on South Mountain, and of current
belief there.

Our first secret is a very fascinating one, and of such
incalculable importance to all society belles that we trust
to receive from them at least, unlimited acknowledgment
of gratitude, rare as this virtue is in the world.

We also deem its promulgation an important accessory to all æsthetic drawing-rooms, where it is expected that all ugly people shall absent themselves, inasmuch as their presence would essentially mar the worship of the beautiful. We are now taught by the Renaissance movement that no necessity exists for the slightest blot or spot or imperfection on the fair face of Nature; that it is the perfect mission of the Modern Hellenist to produce forms of the beautiful everywhere, forms in which there is the perfect repose of harmonious combination. This development will produce an ecstatic commingling and intermingling of all that is graceful. Thus no glaring effects shall be permitted to startle the exquisitely sensitive appreciation, and ethereal nothings shall be accepted as realities.

We are taught that the tear of the Peri is something too, too utterly material to be endurable; that positively all the odious forms of upholstery that made our ancestors have straight backs and square methods must give way to Hogarth's sinuous line of limitless flexibility.

We are told, moreover, that the ingrate who is so shameless as to be poor when surrounded by the beautiful made manifest in forms that he can gaze upon, must nevertheless cease and desist from being low-bred; *par example*, if said impecuniosity is compelled to drink water from an earthen jug, that there is at least no reason why this very primitive utensil should not conform in its molding to Grecian outlines. There must always, no matter how mean the uses or adaptations, exist classic forms. The age demands that the universal perception of the æsthetic shall rise to the zenith of sublimated vaporousness, and that no man shall live and be tolerated, even though he be starving, who shall be so inane as, when placed in presence of the Grecian perfection of form, or of Elia's roast pig, shall so sink to the nadir of vulgar taste as to prefer the prolongation of existence and the pig to the beautiful abstraction. *Nous avons changé tout cela,* and no demoiselle must ever again be seen with even the minutest blemish on her face.

We wish it fully understood that it is because we are æsthetic and consistent in our love of the beautiful, that we so generously give away this secret. One of such a nature that, if placed in the hands of a patent agency, would be of more value than Aladdin's fabled lamp as manipulated by the genie. But, wishing to promote the æsthetic movement, we disdain all practical considerations, and are thankful to make known this hidden lore. It is this:

The complexion may be made beautiful and all freckles and spots washed away and a purely æsthetic color procured, by a visit to the dewy fields at sunrise on the first day of May. Kneel in a limp way, *"say the words"* thrice, and bathe the unwashed face three times with dew. Is it not delicious? "The words" mean, to call upon the three Highest Names. We may add, that the fair maiden who confesses to this practice, now has a color of ravishing freshness. She told us that her face at one time was disfigured by black freckles, when she determined to try this charm, and went alone in the field as directed. On her return home she was scarcely recognized, so entirely had those ugly sun-spots been effaced. Nor have they returned. We certainly can attest the present singular beauty of her complexion, and are ready to aver that when she shall reach that plane of intelligence requisite to cultivate the lily in its chaste expressiveness or the sunflower in its leonine strength, she will be as æsthetic as modern *bric-à-brac* or the Queen Anne style of architecture.

We are reluctant to leave a subject so full of alluring sweetness in order to speak of anything so crude and superlatively aciduous as a lemon-tree. But still, as this tree has its uses as furnishing a fruit which is a prophylactic against Washington malaria, we are happy to give any information tending to its preservation.

Having purchased a fine lemon-tree in full bearing, of a well-to-do farmer, it was sent to us with strict injunctions, if we desired that it should continue to flourish, that we must by no means remove "the charms!" These consisted of an old horse-shoe tacked on the tree, and of two small bottles tied to its branches, filled with a liquid closely resembling molasses and water. We are sorry to have to say that our disregard of the advice and the removal of these charms seemed to have a bad effect on the tree, — a circumstance which doubtless will help to enforce the silly observance of this charm with others.

Our next secret is of a domestic nature. If roaches infest your premises, it is considered easy to get rid of them in this way: Wrap two of these bugs in a piece of brown paper, take the parcel to the nearest cross-road where four roads center, "*say the words*" three times. This expression always means to call upon the most holy Trinity. Then lay the roaches down, and the whole tribe that infest your place will emigrate en masse to the neighbor's house nearest the cross-roads. This is often done, and is relied upon. Nor have we heard of any law-suits arising out of this selfish invasion of another's soil, as fond as these people are of "going to the law." As we heard a man say, "I will have my *liar* speak to your *liar.*" We trust that the legal profession will not institute an action against the above rendering; at least, we beg pardon of the strictly veracious jurists whom we have the honor to know.

If plants are endowed with magical properties in the wonder-working Orient, so has South Mountain stones that are equally useful. For instance: if one buys a cow and she is disposed to return to her old home, procure three stones from her former habitat, "*saying the words thrice,*" and place them in her new barn-yard. You will thus establish another Lares and Penates for Madam Bovine, and she will consequently be made to feel at home. The farmer's wife who told me this "secret" has never had any trouble from erratic cows since using this barn-yard magnet.

But when your hens are disposed to be peripathetic, and wandering away, make their nests in strange places, so that the eggs cannot be found, one must wait as patiently as may be until the next Shrove-Tuesday. Be then on the alert, and by peep-o'-day describe a circle on the ground large enough to enclose your poultry. Place in the center of this circle some corn; then call, "chick, chick," and when all are enclosed in the circle, even to the last straggler, walk round the magic ring three times, each time pronouncing the three Highest Names. You may then be sure of faithful and discreet hens for that year. This "charm," was told us, as a secret, by a very successful adept in the poultry business. But it must be renewed each year. Chanticleer is not included; no way having as yet been invented to keep him at home. The learned will kindly take notice of the gap thus left open to the explorations of the *savant*, and at least supply a theory!

It would be well also to make the "spell" work more than one year at a time with the hens, if possible.

A farmer's wife, who speaks of the writer as Miss Green, who lives at "ye ould tavern oup on ye hill," is not a little worried because an "evil eye" has bewitched her cow, — one of three she owns. She says this evil eye acts like an evil hand and milks her cow dry, so that she no longer gives her milk. As we were one day driving past her house, she ran out to stop the carriage, begging us to speak to "the witch" "to take the spell off."

Another neighbor has fared worse. The evil eye has evil tongue, and in anger says, "I wish your cow may die upon her knee." A few days after the utterance of this threat, the cow was found dead in the field upon her knee. Then this calamity was thus solemnly announced to the witch: "Come, now, and see your cow, she has died upon her knee."

But the most distressing case of mischief, attributed to the Evil Eye, is the Wild Man. Poor wild man! They say his antics are produced by the spell the Evil Eye has laid upon him. He has been the terror of the South Mountain women, who cross these almost pathless forests alone; for he has but one harrowing word, which he shouts in clarion notes, whenever he sees a woman as a war cry! It is, "Petticoats"!! We have courageously interviewed the accused Evil Eye (said eye being a decided case of strabismus), and asked, "why she did so cruel a thing as to set this poor man crazy." She laughed derisively and, looking at us asquint, said, "And is it not known that three-fourths of the world are fools?" "Well, then!" we reply. "Well, then!" she repeats. "*There* is your answer!" Then, after a pause, she added: "I will explain just how it came to pass. The so-called wild man was once sensible enough. He loved one of our mountain girls, and she loved him. But her parents would never hear to the match, and finally she married another man, and so he went crazy, and the poor fool is now in an insane asylum. I had no hand in it."

This same witch has become our good friend, and we have purchased of her various of her secrets. She knows and practices eleven cures, and we have nearly all of them. We will mention them all, in strict confidence, to our dear reader. It may be supposed that these cures are fabrications, but this is not so. They were related to us *bona-fide*. First we have the shingles, a sort of erysipelas, called also St. Anthony's fire, and not an uncommon form of disease among the mountaineers. To cure shingles you must procure a brand of hickory fire. The burning coal must absolutely be of hickory; no other wood will have the needed virtue in it. Hold it in your hand, encircle the extent of the eruption three times with the coal, and repeat each time, in the three Highest Names, "*Wild fire*, move away while the *tame fire* is over you. Shingles, move away in the three Highest Names." We are told that this incantation never fails. The "wild fire" is noticed to pale at once, and will often entirely disappear in a few hours. There would seem to be an occult meaning in the difference of essence between wild and tame fire which is curious — *wild* evidently means *evil*, or, rather, the evil spirit.

Second cure. — *The Go-Backs*. This very retrogressive name is given to a sort of atrophy which often attacks children crowded in these huts, and produces a state of inanition or wasting away. For this sickness the following is considered a famous remedy, and is a real secret, which makes it all the more delightful to tell: —

To cure the "go-backs" take two strings, and here, at the very start, candor compels us to mention that the doctors are at variance. Some assert that these strings should be woolen, while others insist that cotton should be used! But as each school equally attains success, we opine that, like more abstruse philosophic methods that differ, either will answer. We are reminded of the old logic so well thumbed at school, making tweedle-dum prove tweedle-dee. "When doctors disagree, who shall decide?" Which shall it be, cotton or wool? Taking, then, the two strings, with one string measure the patient from the crown of the head to the tip of the toes, while the other string must be used in this way: Extend the arms in the form of a cross, and measure from tips of fingers across. This second measurement has a double purpose, and is used as a diagnostic of the disease, namely, if the patient measures more cross-wise than length-wise, it is for certain the "*abnehmen.*" This is the secret name for "go-backs."

The grandmother of a very sick baby told us with great concern, that the child measured one inch too much cross-wise, and that the spell was working wrong. Nine days is the time given to decide how the cure will work. After the measurement, grease the patient three times, well down the breast-bone and on the ribs, using the two thumbs for this manipulation; and, while you grease, keep saying these "words" three times in the three Highest Names, "*Abnehmen, depart.*" This done, take the door of the room off its hinges, and twist one of the two strings, each on a hinge. Then, rehang the door, and when the action of the door shall wear these strings by the ordinary course of opening and shutting, the child will be cured. We fear that we cannot sufficiently impress the chosen ones who have the privilege of reading this erudite work, with a just appreciation of the value attached to this method of cure. Patients have been brought to South Mountain by scores in order to reap the benefit to be derived from its application! Mothers have assured us that it has saved their children when the doctors were unsuccessful. It has always been performed with a certain mystery. The little sufferer was taken away from its parent or nurse, and laid upon a bed in a dark room, quite alone with the wizard. It is not very dignified, perhaps, to make confession as to the source of our knowledge, but it was gained in a very simple way. Our informant peeped through the crack of the wonderful door, and thus learned the manner of operating.

And this reminds us that the discovery of a cure for feminine curiosity might be an object worthy of the attention of the most learned men, or indeed of being referred to the investigations of the medical profession en masse. In fact, statistics on the subject are requested as tending to establish data of importance. We humbly hint, also, that our mathematicians will doubtless be able to trace an interesting proof of the principle of inverse or reciprocal ratio, in the peculiar manner of this cure; namely, in proportion as the strings waste away, so the patient revives! This occult law is here so beautifully exemplified, that in its application to the resuscitation of vital force, we would suggest the founding of a new school of medicine to be called Ratio-pathic, or the Ratio-nal! We take it for granted that the enlightened public desires to elaborate and utilize all suggestions of value propounded for its consideration.

We crave pardon of the fastidious, but our cure number three is — for a boil or *imposthüme* — or as our hamlet Esculapius calls it — "a bile."

Describe a circle three times with the thumb of the right hand, round the exterior circumference of the tumor, and repeat each time in the three Highest Names, this verse:

> "The Dragon and the Bile,
> Went over the Creek,
> And the Dragon drunk,
> And the Bile Thunk."

The hypercritical may exclaim, as we did, "Thunk!"
"You mean sunk, doubtless." "Not at all," replied the
Witch of Endor, "I mean Thunk." So in spite of Murray's
ghost, Thunk it shall be. Will the antiquarians of the
country please discover if this word can be traced to the
Egyptian Sphinx, or is it merely an Anglo-Saxon or
Druidical *root*? We have a vague impression that
perchance it may be one of those mutterings, which
were so unintelligible, of the Delphian Pythoness; or a
deciphered Egyptian hieroglyphic; or has been used to
describe the predictive visions of augurs, for it could
scarcely be descriptive of aerial *simulacra,* where the
"imagination bodies forth the forms of things unseen,"
— and the tongue invents words unknown.

Our fourth cure is very valuable to sporting men.
To cure bots, stand the sick horse with his head towards
the east or, as the French say, let him *s'orienter.* Then
measure him with a string, from the tip of his nose,
down over his back, to the end of his tail, and say three
times over him, in the three Highest Names," these
words, which we do not recommend for the versification:

"A man rode over the land
With three worms in his hand,
The one was white,
The one was black,
And the other was red.
And in an hour they are all dead."

Our informant once cured a horse of bots in the old
stable of South-Mountain-House, when it is averred that
he "staggered" so, that he had to be held up while the
measure was being taken. The animal at once rose to the
level of the occasion, and resumed its daily work;
although, for all we know, it may by this time, like the
aforesaid worms, be likewise dead.

There is thought to be so much pure charlatanism
about "horse doctors," that we confess that we have fears
as to the permanency of this cure. However, it will be

well for our army men to investigate it, in order to economize for the United States as far as possible, in fact, it is their duty so to do. We feel called upon to speak plainly. One more suggestion in this connection. There is a quaint English verse that runs thus:

> "A worm or maggot in the head
> Of the most subtle man is bred:
> Wise men, at some odd hours, we see,
> Have some short fits of lunacy,
> And every skull, all must confess,
> Has a soft place in 't, more or less."

Now, perhaps, this "bee in the bonnet" may be of the same species as those "the man rode over the land" with. And this is a subject which our naturalists should not overlook. We expect them to "classify" these white, black, red, and brainy myths. The latter are said at times to grow as big as a "hobby-horse." But Heaven forfend that such an abnormal growth should afflict any of our readers.

The cures numbers five and six are so similar, that they may be classed together. They are for the specific diseases called heart's bound and liver grown, proving to our mind that an unjaundiced eye will herein see a close sympathy between these organs. In this cure, take the patient, grease down the breastbone and round the ribs with the two thumbs three times, saying, "Move and depart from my child's ribs, as our Jesus did from His manger, in the three Highest Names." There is one Mountain old woman, who follows a somewhat different method, which we reserve until we shall have received an honorary diploma to practice witch-magic on South Mountain. And this to be awarded by a liberal-minded Faculty. In fact, the concurrent experience of mankind goes to prove that "silence is golden," and we do not intend to tell in one book *all* that we know, — no, not even to the dear Public.

Perhaps our oculists may not be aware that a film over

the eye can be disposed of in this manner: it is the mystical *seventh* cure. Say, "Eye, I do not know what ails you, I know not whence it is. There shall it go, in the name of the Trinity. Amen." Then rub the eye three times with the right hand, and repeat three times. So will it depart.

This may be called "special" practice. Here is another for a cataract of the eye. Say, "I rub you with my right thumb, that you must move, and depart in the three Highest Names. Amen." Then rub it with the thumb three times, from the nose, until you say the above words, then blow three times; then say these words three times morning and evening, on every morning and every evening three times. We know of a man who had consulted doctors in vain for an inflamed eye, who actually was cured by this nonsense in two or three days.

A farm-hand, working for a friend of ours, preferred the following for a scalded hand to any of the doctor's remedies: it is magic cure number eight. If a person burns or scalds himself, say, "The holy woman went over the land. What carries she in her hand? *A firebrand.* Eat not in you, fire! — eat not around you, fire! In the three Highest Names. Amen." Then say these words, and rub three times with the right hand upwards and downwards over the part three times, and blow three times – each time three times. There is, of a certainty, a full measure of credulity needed to perfect these cures, — yet they are in vogue. We give them as they have been made known to us. The mystical number *nine* is the following, for what they called *night-brand,* or *scrofula:* "I forewarn you, that you shall no longer burn, but be you cold as a dead man's hand." Then say, in the three Highest Names, and after that take the middle finger of the right hand, and rub three times around, over, and underneath, morning and evening. Each time repeat the foregoing words three times.

Whenever, in any of these invocations, a name is used, it should always be the Christian name, or if a woman, also the maiden name in addition.

For the tenth cure, called by these people *falling-fit,* or *falling-sickness,* or the epilepsy. Take a broom, and sweep from three corners of the room, and throw the sweepings over the person that has the sickness, saying, "Here I sow this seed in God's name: falling-disease, you must depart, till I these seeds do cut." This must be repeated three times in the "three Highest Names." The last cure, which completes the circle of the *répertoire* of the Mountain Witch, is for *dropsy.* When we shall have learned these magic words, we may make our readers, in the second edition of this work, the custodians of our acquisitions. An old woman told us, that being at death's door with dropsy, she was cured by the magic words and the following prescription. The words were withheld from us, but the prescription was given. Although we give it as a country remedy, we do not advise any one to try it, for, so far as we know, it may be quite as likely to kill as cure. All we can say is, that the doctress who gave it to us, considers it a secret remedy of great importance. For the dropsy she said, — Take 3 pints of vinegar, 1 oz. Juniper berries, 1 oz. squills, 1 gill mustard-seed, 1 handful parsley root, 2 handsful of horseradish root. Mix together, and boil down to one quart, in an iron pot. Take three wine glassful during the day, one before each meal.

Theologians will observe, that in all these cures there is an implied blasphemy in the allusion or making direct use of the invocation of the Most Holy Trinity.

Our own conviction is, that if there are surprising results, as asserted, that both *the power and the sin* rest in this sacrilege. The rest is, of course, as stupid as the African fetichism. Invariably when these magic cures are told to us, we ask, "And how do you cure?" We are answered, "By words." "What are these words?" We find them always in some way connected with the "three Highest Names." When we again ask, — "But why always repeat *three* times, and why call upon these sacred Names?" The answer is always to shake the head, and say, *"We can do nothing without them."*

We have been told, that Granny M—e had a tooth that

hurt her, and she sent word to a witch-conjurer to "say the words," and pull it out. This was done in effect, the operator being *three miles distant* from the scene of his operations!!! By an act of the will directed with the intention of extracting the tooth, and *saying the words* with this object in view! We have to exclaim with the Dominie, — Pro-di-gi-ous! One can readily imagine what an immense practice such an adroit manipulator would have in our cities. Perchance, this effective magnetic extraction may be one of the wonders reserved for the age succeeding the telephone? How delightful and æsthetic to send a dreamy message, "Pull my teeth and give me a new set"! The chords vibrate, now and then, perchance, a sentiment of discord pervades the system. Then is syllabled the inspiriting response, "Madam, you are rejuvenated"!! O, happy twentieth century!

But we may not linger amid these pleasing reveries, for we hear our crone crooning. There are still other things to consider, Horatio, not as yet known to thy philosophy. The occult words are also connected with charms in use for the cure of bee, wasp, and hornet stings, as well as to counteract the venom of snakes. An odd case was told us, of a baby that was supposed to be dying, and was taken to a "witch-conjurer" for treatment.

A pinch of flour and water was placed three times, in the three Highest Names, on the temples, breast, and backbone of the infant. Whereupon a multitude of minute black heads appeared. Then these worms were shaved away with a razor.

Another case was narrated, where a child being very ill, the breast was greased three times, saying the words; when thousands of little worms appeared, that werc omb-ed off. This story of the thaumaturgist combing out worms, is, after all, not more incredible than one of Plutarch's descriptions; for this writer mentions, that near the Red Sea are seen creeping from the bodies of diseased people, a multitude of little snakes. It is passing strange, how varied are the legends, of all climes, all nations, and all ages, that have found a congenial home on South Mountain.

"In winter's tedious night, sit by the fire,
With these old folk, and let them tell thee tales."

And, as thou listenest, and the Storm King rises from his lair, thou wilt hear innumerous voices make wild response. They answer back from crisp meadow, from moaning forest, from whispering cave, and from rugged rocks, from cliff re-echoing back to cliff. And bold indeed is the courage that dares the hurtling tempest, and brave is the heart that sees the conflict and knows no quickened throb. The crooning winter's tale dies out with the expiring glow on the deep old hearth-stone, as the dying embers throw out fantastic shapes, that glare, flicker, and glimmer again. We feel that at the "witching hour," the elfish dance must commence, and that we are in an atmosphere of optical illusions and strange delusions. The moods that beset us here are not to be measured by conventional standards.

Of the various hair-breadth escapes, that of snake stories is a favorite theme on this Mountain. As the ancients believed that the basilisk and the asp caused death by their poisonous breath, so they tell one of "blowing viper," *with a hood.* A man killed one on the cliff back of South-Mountain-House, but was afraid to approach near, and shot it at a distance. This hooded serpent is very unpleasantly suggestive of the dreaded cobra-de-capello of the Indies.

An old woman told us that the snake the mountaineers most dreaded was the hoop; but that this kind was so very rarely met with that, although she had lived in the woods all her life, she had never seen but one. If one-tenth the terrors with which her imagination invested this serpent are true, or indeed, if there is such a serpent at all, the presence of even one in a forest would be about as formidable as that of the fabled flying Dragon. Her description, however, may serve to amuse, if not to instruct. She says that "the hoop snake puts its tail in its mouth, when in pursuit of its victim, and rolls on with an incredible rapidity. The reptile wears a horn on its head, *and kills whatever it touches!*"

On the one memorable occasion of her life when she saw the "hoop," she was walking with Moses and a female friend. They were ascending the Pinnacle, when they saw something green spread out at length upon the sward. While they stood curiously looking at it, suddenly it put its tail in its mouth, raised its horn, and began to roll. "Look out for yourselves, women," shouted Moses; "it's a regular hoop!" They sprang to a rail fence that happily was near, and as it gave chase, they had scarcely time to swiftly climb the rails, when it shot by. It rolled down the green meadow, and as it passed on, its slimy track could readily be scanned by the desolation. Once it struck a living tree, and the beauteous foliage shrunk and withered, and in two hours the verdurous mass was dead! This terrible serpent, as here described by an illiterate country woman, is but a repetition of the monsters that were said to spread such dismay and ruin that half the romances of knightly exploits were based upon the glory of their destruction. We willingly leave this particular one to speed its deadening circles down into Dante's Inferno, where it will doubtless find its proper place, only asking that it may never again inhabit South Mountain.

Of other snakes, the black snake is of several varieties, and grows to a large size, especially the Racer, which, as its name betokens, is swift to movement. The country people avoid it by pursuing a zig-zag course when chased, and even the children can elude its rapid pursuit.

We have heard the large kind of black snakes, that are at times shot at in the trees, and whose power consists in the strength of the constrictive folds in which they enwrap their victim, called boa-constrictors. We were surprised to hear a name applied whose use it was to be supposed ignorance would have prevented; for there certainly is a strong family resemblance. These snakes would rather seem to seek the companionship of people, for they certainly do not avoid inhabited places, as do other snakes.

A woman told us that, walking up the Mountain canyon one bright moonlight night, she felt something tugging at her dress. She walked on for some time without giving the matter much thought, until a nearer rustling noise caused her to look around, when she saw two large black snakes clinging to the hem of her dress. She was compelled, as she expressed it, "to give battle," in order to shake them off.

There is no doubt but that snakes are attracted or repulsed by certain influences. It is of common belief, for instance, that to burn shoe leather will drive snakes away. Such is the current opinion. But we have never heard any theory broached, only the fact mentioned.

Speaking of *theories*, we cannot refrain from narrating an absurd instance. One bright morning, on South Mountain, we were accosted by a woman who, with a perplexed air, said she had "a theory" she would like our opinion about. It was this, — that the very tedious journey to China might, it seemed to her, be taken in one day. Since the world hung in space like a ball, she suggested that one might rise in a balloon until one could hang suspended over *the other side* of this sphere, then drop right down — presto — quick — on the Chinese!

We hope that the reader will pardon us for tolerating this nascent theorist, with whom "a little knowledge was a dangerous thing." But it is impossible to give an idea of the gravity of this "theory," unless one had seen the solemnity with which it was propounded.

We shall now, in conclusion, speak of a series of extraordinary delusions. The High Priest of all this evil practice, for mere mummery it can scarcely be called, was the old man Michael Zittle, who died in the summer of 1877. He was resorted to by hundreds of people from all the country round about South Mountain, and even from a distance, many of whom went away in the belief

that they had been cured; and they may have been so.
He is said, when dying, to have transferred "his power"
to a member of his family, to whom he also left his book.

The methods of cure of this thaumaturgist were made
according to this work on the Black Art. It is very
curious that, like the Black-Book of the *Baschkirs*, it
should descend by choice with the power conferred.

A friend of ours, who had an attack of ophthalmia, on
South Mountain, which deprived her for six weeks of all
use of her eyes, received repeated messages from this
man that he could cure her if she would allow him to
"say the words" over her. She now experiences regret
that she did not at least see the old wizard and converse
with him, as he died some weeks later; and it is said that
he expired in great agony of soul, and without any of the
consolations or succors which religion alone can bring
at this supreme hour. He lived not a mile from South
Mountain House.

The relative to whom Zittle left his book and his
"power" is now also dead; and although several persons
still claim to work cures by means of "words," we are
not aware of the extent of their claims, or what degree of
credence is given to them.

A very remarkable scene is said to have transpired
after the death of Summers, the son-in-law of Zittle,
upon whom the "power" of Zittle was alleged to have
descended. Mr. Summers died at the age of forty, of
consumption. After his death, it became necessary to
put cotton in his nostrils, ears, and mouth, and in this
condition he was duly buried. Some days after the
funeral, his widow, who was a daughter of Michael Zittle,
the so-called "wizard," was informed of the circumstance
about the cotton, and she became greatly agitated and
alarmed in consequence. She asserted that if the dead
man should swallow the least portion of this cotton, the
entire family, and even his friends, would of necessity
die. To allay her fears and anguish of mind, and possibly
because the apprehensions of the relatives were aroused,
the body was resurrected in order to displace the cotton.

It was thought by others that, had this precaution been neglected, some convulsion of nature, that might have shaken old South Mountain from summit to base, must have occurred!!

This almost incredible outbreak of superstition took place, if we are not mistaken, in the summer of 1877. Can it be wondered at, that all manner of signs and omens are scrupulously consulted? That ghosts, hobgoblins, and fairies are believed to exist? that the ordinary events of life, the planting, sowing, plowing, reaping, the days to work, the days to desist from work, the placing sunflowers round the cabins to keep off witches, the cutting of finger-nails on Saturday, and a thousand similar beliefs, should all be considered with exact care? Doubtless the long-continued practices of the old "wizard," as many called him, had much to do with this state of affairs.

We have seen the original "Conjuring-Book" of Old Zittle. It is in German, and we have made a rude translation of portions of its sibylline leaves, quite enough of it, we trust, to satisfy the curiosity of our learned readers, and more than enough of it to satisfy ourselves as to its true nature.

It is intended as a treatise of so-called "black art," and portions of it are too blasphemous to give a rendering.

We would not, indeed, call the attention of the reader to the book, except in connection with the number of cures said to have been performed through its agency, and believed in as true; and also other results that have followed its use and are narrated as real. When we view it in this sense, it becomes a factor of some interest, as the instrument of a wide-spread superstition. We are told that so long as the old curemonger *refused to take money* his cures were certain; but that later in life, being old and very poor, he was persuaded to ask a fee, and that when he did so, he had "bad luck."

Among all those of this family and others on this mountain who now "try for" (that is the term used) diseases, none have been so fortunate. He called the "go-backs" "*abnehmen*," and had great success in curing this malady.

As this man worked his cures in great part according to the directions given in his book, we wish to explain a little. Wherever the cross (+) is printed, it means to call upon the most Holy Trinity. Indeed, it seems to us that an impious use of holy names and sacrilegious allusions to the sufferings of the Savior form the substance, or warp and woof of the system.

This fact makes us believe that, if direct results of this agency were really obtained as claimed, the power that gave them efficacy was in its nature satanic. It is not our purpose to assert any doctrine in this connection, whatever personal belief we may and do hold, for this is a narrative only, of South-Mountain magic.

The book we have spoken of bears the title of "The Friend in Need; or, Secret Science." The title page simply asserts that it is a translation from the Spanish into German, and states, "Printed for the Purchaser, 1826." It has no publisher's name nor place of printing given: in fact, *no clew* by which any one in Germany could have been held amenable for violation of law in its publication. The preface mentions that the book is written "according to the secret tricks found in an ancient Spanish manuscript herein brought out, which was discovered by an old hermit over a hundred years ago, hidden among the mysteries of the Holy Land; many wonders having thereby been performed in this same country. It also treats of 'The Dragon with Four Young,' etc., etc., ... and it contains rare prescriptions from legends found in Freyburg in 1752," etc., etc.

The first five of its conjurations are for the recovery of stolen property. We shall give one or two headings only and a summary, Number 1 being, "A True Way to discover the Hiding-Place of a Thief or Thieves."

These words are in substance a form calling upon the thief or thieves thrice, in the most Holy Names, to come forth. Number 2 we give entire. It reads thus: "How One may compel a Thief or Thieves to restore Stolen

Property." "O thief or thieves, lay down what thou hast stolen and go away, *in Satan's name*, in whose name thou hast taken my property."

It will be conceded that this form at least is an invocation or diabolism pure and simple.

Number 3: "How to proceed when a Thief or Thieves have stolen a Horse." Take the pitch-fork and stick where the horse stood. Call the horse by name, and say: 'I trample thee, I stick thee, I bite thee. Thou shalt come back and thou shalt turn the thief's hand quickly, even as the wind or the fish that swim in the water or the birds that fly in the woods, or else thou shalt lie low under the sod. Come quick and be swift."

Number 4 tells "How to proceed when one has been robbed:" "Take three nails, in the name of God. Throw away the first nail, and while doing so call upon the thief to restore that which he has stolen, or else he will meet with the fate of Judas." Here imprecations are added. When the second nail is cast down similar threats are made, and when the third nail is thrown, call upon the most Holy Trinity, and add imprecations still more dreadful. This is a very long form, and we have only given its general scope.

One conjuration is headed, "How to make one's self *invisible*." This form is too impious for repetition.

Then we have, "A Sure Cure for Fever." After this a number of cures for what these people call "blood stopping." This cure is believed to cause an immediate cessation of the flow of blood from a wound, and one of our neighbors is said to have had his life saved in the following manner: The man, when intoxicated, accidentally gave himself a fearful gash with an axe. They ran for the "granny" *to say the words*, which words were no sooner pronounced than the gushing of blood ceased.

When blood flows the method is peculiar, for no matter how imminent the danger, they first pause and carefully wrap up and lay away the instrument that caused the wound. This is evidently a wise precaution, and, although taken rather late, cannot be objected to, but these people attach a secret significance to the act.

There is a form, "How to close a wound from fire-arms," but it is too blasphemous for utterance, as it claims its power by an invocation of the sacred blood of Christ, of the five precious wounds, and of the most Holy Trinity.

A French gentleman, who is now no more, but who was of the highest culture, observing this superstitious practice, while making us a visit at South Mountain, mentioned that near Marseilles, in France, some very degraded peasants make use of a similar impiety with a view to the stopping a flow of blood from a wound, and with acknowledged favorable results.

The little book of which we write has eight forms for the healing of wounds, each applicable to a hurt of a different nature, as when caused by violence in a quarrel from fire-arms or from cuts. But the forms are one and all sacrilegious, and in substance repeat each other.

There is but one spell that makes use of numbers, and these numbers have an occult meaning wholly unintelligible to us. We shall give the entire form.

It is possible that these letters and numbers may be connected with some method of finding a numerical magic square, or with Astrological divinations.

This spell is headed, "How to stop the flowing of blood for one's self." Say, "In God's heart stop," 3, 2, 8g. 28 these are his, t59 28d, these others also are his. 5, 865, 28d, the third is his wish. Stop, blood, stop. So must thou surely stop. So God be praised. Bb 5t 7622 5th h 1tg 261 B 28. + + +.

Some of the prescriptions in the book remind one of the Zingari lore. The following is one, which is evidently intended to be mesmeric in its nature, and seems to be a sort of gypsy trick. It is, "How to make a dog willing to stay with you." Take a small piece of bread, lay it under the shoulder until it is warm, and give the dog to eat; or, take a laurel leaf, give the dog half of it, and keep the other half yourself.

The next reminds one of some pagan rite. It is,

"How to dispel fear of the darkness of night." Take water which is distilled, and mix with man's blood, spread it over the face, and thou wilt fear nothing. Thou mayest go wherever thou wilt."

If one wishes always to win at cards use the following spell: "Bind the heart of a bat round the arm that deals the cards with a red silk thread." We suppose this is of course connected with some superstition about that uncanny *lusus naturæ* — the bat.

There is one of real witchcraft, but our rather limited command of the German language prevented our understanding the conjuration, and we were only permitted to retain the book a few days, during which we had to decipher its contents as best we could, unassisted by books of reference.

The way in which we happened to see the original book was quite accidental. We called to see an old woman who was considered "a doctress." She was ill, and we found her much troubled because some one had robbed her. But she said that she was trying the various conjurations of the "black book" with the expectation of discovering the thief, and thus being able to regain her stolen property. She mentioned to us that the "wizard" had lent her *the book* for that purpose. We had often heard this book alluded to as the "conjuring book," and were curious to see it, and we obtained a very reluctant consent from this old woman to take it home for a few days only.

The conjuration we last alluded to has for title, "How to divine the time of one's death." Take a very little olive oil, mix it with good brandy, add a little yellow white ingredient (we could not understand this substance), and set fire to the mixture. The vision that will appear from the flames will be so terrible that each one present will *tremble for his neighbor!* This is certainly a rather novel mode of frightening people, and some doubtless would not strongly object to a "vicarious terror."

We close with "A sure trick against fire," which we have been assured is infallible. There are, however, ten more forms for "cures" or "spells" set down, but we have already doubtless overtaxed the patience of our reader and must finish. This art against fire is, however, very peculiar. The book tells us that it can also be used as a protection against lightning. It is likewise a cure for the bite of a mad dog. Make the dog eat the words, and he can do no harm. This advice is suggestive of the joke so often put upon children, namely, to catch a bird by putting salt upon its tail, which is doubtless less difficult than to make any rabid dog eat these twenty-five letters. Any one who was to try to enforce the remedy would, we opine, be in danger of the contagious virus. As a remedy for fever the treatment is easy, for the patient will be cured if the words are laid under his back for twenty-four hours. It says: Persist in these twenty-five spells as used in the following table which observe well. These twenty-five letters form the hymn which the three men Shadrach, Meshach, and Abednego did sing when the king Nebuchadnezzar threw them in the fiery furnace. These twenty-five letters are the spell through which they induced God to send his holy angel to keep them in safety in the midst of their distress. They also preserved Daniel in the lion's den.

Whosoever shall have this hymn in his possession, or in his house, will be safe: his house shall be secure from fire, thunder, or lightning. The magic letters are as follows, and are of precisely the same mysterious import as the *Abracadabra*, so familiar to all magicians.

S	A	T	O	R
A	R	E	T	O
T	E	S	E	T
O	T	E	R	A
R	O	T	A	S

It will readily be observed that these twenty-five "spells" or "letters" form a magic square, namely, a series of letters disposed in parallel and equal ranks; so that the letters of each row, taken perpendicularly and horizontally, form a repetition, and the reverse obtains. When taken diagonally they have some reference one to the other.

These squares, as is well known, astrologers consider as planetary and talismanic. They use them in casting horoscopes and in predicting the future. While sorcerers probably ascribe to them, also, certain virtues; as, in this case, belonging to a similar disposition of letters and figures. Nor can it be said that the various arts by which horoscopes are cast, and future events foretold, are no longer in vogue; for one has only to glance over the advertising columns of the daily journals in our large cities to observe what a number of avowed charlatans exist upon the credulity of society.

Dr. Franklin thought it worth while, as a matter of mathematical investigation, to speculate upon the magic square; and, the result of his studies formed a very elaborate one.

In conclusion, whatever deception, illusion, imposition, or diablerie outright, our recital may include, the narrative of these practices is quite true, as narrated to us, and is a collection of traditions received by our narrators as facts.

We, in turn, submit these superstitions to the curious speculations of the learned, and to the judgment of the wise.

We know that in the alembic of well-directed science, loose analogies and faint resemblances must disappear, and the arcana of nature be made to yield her pure grain of truth.

The golden thread which connects the ages cannot be destroyed.

And, finally, we must say, that personally we feel very much relieved at having been able to tell so many "*secrets,*" in strict confidence, to such a select circle as our readers form of our very particular and intimate friends.

Printed in the USA
CPSIA information can be obtained
at www.ICGtesting.com
LVHW041530280723
753393LV00004B/758